LETTERS TO THE NEW ISLAND

W. B. YEATS AT THE AGE OF 23

From a portrait by H. M. Paget in the Belfast Art Gallery

LETTERS TO THE NEW ISLAND

BY

WILLIAM BUTLER YEATS

EDITED WITH AN INTRODUCTION

BY

HORACE REYNOLDS

CAMBRIDGE, MASSACHUSETTS

HARVARD UNIVERSITY PRESS

These Essays of William Butler Yeats are reprinted
by permission of *The Boston Pilot* and
The Providence Journal

FIRST PUBLISHED 1934
REPRINTED 1970

PRINTED LITHOGRAPHICALLY IN GREAT BRITAIN
AT THE UNIVERSITY PRESS, OXFORD
BY VIVIAN RIDLER
PRINTER TO THE UNIVERSITY

CONTENTS

*"Was man in der Jugend wünscht,
hat man im Alter die Fülle."*

OLD GERMAN PROVERB

PREFACE

WHILE I was lecturing somewhere in the Eastern States Mr. Reynolds sent me a bundle of photographic copies of articles of mine published in American newspapers when I was a very young man, said they would interest students of the Irish intellectual movement and asked leave to publish them. I thought his letter generous, for all but two or three had been published before the Copyright Act of 1891. I read what was not too blurred or in too small print for my sight, and noticed that I had in later life worked out with the excitement of discovery things known in my youth as though one forgot and rediscovered oneself. I had forgotten my early preoccupation with the theatre, with an attempt to free it from commercialism with a handsome little stage in a Bedford Park Clubhouse. As

I read, Florence Farr's acting in Todhunter's *Sicilian Idyll* came into my
mind, her beautiful speaking, the beautiful
speaking of Heron Allen, cheiromantist
and authority upon old violins, the poor
acting and worse speaking of some woman
engaged from some London theatre. Two
or three times in later life I made, as I
thought for the first time, the discovery
made in that little theatre that the highly
cultivated man or woman can in certain
kinds of drama surpass an actor who is
in all things save culture their superior.
Since then my friends and I have created
a theatre famous for its " folk art," for its
realistic studies of life, but done little for
an other art that was to come, as I hoped,
out of modern culture where it is most
sensitive, profound and learned. In these
articles I overrated Dr. Todhunter's poetical importance, not because he was a
friendly neighbour with a charming house,
a Morris carpet on the drawing-room
floor, upon the walls early pictures by

my father painted under the influence of
Rossetti, but because a single play of his,
the *Sicilian Idyll* — I did not overrate
the rest of his work — and still more its
success confirmed a passion for that other
art. When Shelley wrote *The Cenci* — it
had just been played for the first time —
when Tennyson wrote *Beckett*, they were,
I argued with Todhunter, deliberately
oratorical; instead of creating drama in
the mood of *The Lotus Eaters* or of *Epi-
psychidion* they had tried to escape their
characteristics, had thought of the theatre
as outside the general movement of literature. That he might keep within it I had
urged upon Todhunter a pastoral theme,
and had myself begun *The Countess Cathleen*, avoiding every oratorical phrase and
cadence. A few months before I had seen
George Macdonald and his family play in
the Bedford Park Clubhouse a dramatised
version of the *Pilgrim's Progress* before
hangings of rough calico embroidered in
crewel work, and thought that some like

method might keep the scenery from realism. I should have added that to avoid
the suggestions of the press that bring all
things down to the same level, we should
play before an audience vowed to secrecy.
I spent my life among painters who hated
the Royal Academy, popular art, fashion-
able life. I could remember some painter
saying in my childhood, " Holman Hunt
will never come to anything, I have just
heard that he gets his dress clothes at
Poole's " — Poole was the most fashion-
able of all tailors. When I had founded
the Irish Literary Society and gone to
Ireland to found a similar society there I
had all the fanaticism of the studios. The
article that interests me most is that written in the Dublin National Library, where
everybody was working for some examina-
tion, nobody, as I thought, for his own
mind's sake or to discover happiness.
New rules have compelled the students to
go elsewhere for their school books, but
Irish education is still commercialised.

I can remember myself sitting there at the age of twenty-six or twenty-seven looking with scorn at those bowed heads and busy eyes, or in futile revery listening to my own mind as if to the sounds in a sea shell. I remember some old man, a stranger to me, saying, " I have watched you for the past half hour and you have neither made a note nor read a word." He had mistaken the proof sheets of "The Works of William Blake, edited and interpreted by Edwin Ellis and William Butler Yeats," for some school or university text book, me for some ne'er-do-weel student. I am certain that everybody outside my own little circle who knew anything about me thought as did that cross old man, for I was arrogant, indolent, excitable. To-day, knowing how great were the odds, I watch over my son, a boy at the preparatory school, fearing that he may grow up in my likeness.

I knew Blake thoroughly, I had read much Swedenborg, had only ceased my

study of Boehme for fear I might do
nothing else, had added a second fanaticism to my first. My isolation from ordinary men and women was increased by an
asceticism destructive of mind and body,
combined with an adoration of physical
beauty that made it meaningless. Sometimes the barrier between myself and other
people filled me with terror; an unfinished
poem, and the first and never-finished
version of *The Shadowy Waters* had this
terror for their theme. I had in an extreme
degree the shyness — I know no better word
— that keeps a man from speaking his
own thought. Burning with adoration
and hatred I wrote verse that expressed
emotions common to every sentimental
boy and girl, and that may be the reason
why the poems upon which my popularity
has depended until a few years ago were
written before I was twenty-seven. Gradually I overcame my shyness a little,
though I am still struggling with it and
cannot free myself from the belief that it

comes from lack of courage, that the problem is not artistic but moral. I remember saying as a boy to some fellow student in the Dublin art schools, " The difference between a good draftsman and a bad is one of courage." I wrote prose badly, *The Celtic Twilight*, written before I had finished the last of the articles in this book, excepted, and that more for its matter than its form; prose, unlike verse, had not those simple forms that like a masquer's mask protect us with their anonymity. Perhaps if he had not been to so much trouble and expense I should have asked Mr. Reynolds to give up his project and yet been sorry afterwards, for these essays, which I have not seen for years, fill me with curiosity.

W. B. Yeats

Dublin
August 1, 1933

INTRODUCTION

INTRODUCTION

I

ONE Monday night in Dublin, six summers ago, four of us set out in a cab from The Bailey to call on Yeats in his house in Merrion Square. At Yeats's we had a rather mixed up evening, everyone cutting across the grain of the others' purposes and desires, but in the course of our talk, Yeats asked me a question which I remembered: "Is a paper I used to write for years ago called The Providence Journal still in existence?"

Several years before this I had happened upon a reference to The Providence Journal in Katharine Tynan's *Twenty-five Years*. I knew that she had written for The Journal: indeed it was Alfred Williams, then editor of that paper, who turned on the tap of her prose and set it flowing; as she herself has said, "Mr. Williams made me begin seriously to write prose." At the time I myself was an occasional contributor to The Journal, and I had meant to look up sometime what my fellow contributor had written forty years before me; but I had never brought myself to the repellent task of handling the very large and very dusty volumes in the newspaper's library.

What Katharine Tynan could not stir me to do, however, Yeats did, and I can still remember the excitement with which I read on the editorial page of The Sunday Journal for May 27, 1888, The Legend of the Phantom Ship, one of the first of Yeats's poems to find the garment of print, and, after it, the five reviews from The Journal here printed. From The Journal the track was well marked to The Boston Pilot — indeed Mr. Allan Wade's bibliography had already pointed out that way — where I found another poem and the fourteen letters to the New Island.

Yeats does not remember how he came to write for The Providence Journal, but it must have been through Alfred Williams, who, in 1887, visited Mrs. Banim, the widow of the Irish novelist, in her house in Dalkey overlooking Dublin Bay.

Doubtless then Mr. Williams, whose interest in Irish letters was keen and early, either met or learned about the young Irish poet who had written *Mosada*. As a memento of this relation, Mr. Williams's books, which on his death he left to the Providence Public Library, contain among other Irish books *The Wanderings of Oisin*, "with the author's compliments," and corrections in the young poet's hand. Yeats says he came to write for The Boston Pilot through John O'Leary, the Fenian. Without doubt O'Leary knew John Boyle O'Reilly, then editor of The Boston Pilot, a fellow Fenian, who, like O'Leary, had suffered imprisonment and exile from Ireland for his political activities.

The first of Yeats's contributions to these two papers was a poem, How Ferencz Renyi Kept Silent, in The Pilot for August 6, 1887; the last, a letter from Dublin in The Pilot for November 19, 1892. Yeats reprinted the two poems, How Ferencz Renyi Kept Silent, and The Phantom Ship, with changes, in *The Wanderings of Oisin*. They are not reprinted here.

These years in London, 1887–1892, belong to a distinct period of Yeats's life; they lap but little over the years 1887–1891, the distinctness of which Yeats recognized when he wrote of them thirty years later under the title *Four Years*. They are the curious, receptive, formative years of a young man of genius in his eager twenties, when he is reading the books, making the friendships, feeling about for the ideas that belong to him, which are later to affect his life. These are the years of Yeats's apprentice work; of the early poems which appeared in the anthologies, *Poems and Ballads of Young Ireland* and *The Book of the Rhymers' Club*; of the volumes of Irish folk and fairy tales and Carleton's stories, which Yeats edited for London publishers; of his first play, *The Countess Cathleen*; of *The Wanderings of Oisin*, his first volume of poems to make a stir among those who cared for poetry.

In these youthful years in London the thin, spectacled, black-coated poet was entering earnestly the life of pen, ink, and paper. Against the advice of his father,

who wanted him to write stories, Yeats
did much critical work and editing. Finally yielding to his father's wishes, he
wrote the story *John Sherman*, whose
background is Sligo and London, pouring
into it, as he did into Innisfree, all his
discontent with London and his nostal-
gia for Ireland. He met Henley and his
young men, he chatted with Lady Wilde
in her drawing-room, and, with his sister,
he joined the circle around William Morris
in the old stable in Hammersmith. Two
of his father's friends, Dr. Todhunter and
T. W. Rolleston, who lived nearby, he influenced to join him in his plans to revive
the poetic drama and make Irish literature national. He met the young men
and women who were to be his friends,
Florence Farr and Maude Gonne, Arthur
Symons, Lionel Johnson, Edwin Ellis,
MacGregor Mathers, Charles Ricketts,
Charles Shannon, and others. He joined
the devotees around Madame Blavatsky's
green baize table; he was initiated into the
Hermetic Students, one of the many societies in which the wave of occult thought
that swept through Great Britain and the

Continent in the eighties manifested itself. With Edwin Ellis he began the work on Blake; with Ernest Rhys he founded the Rhymers' Club, which met nightly for many years at the Cheshire Cheese. There came Lionel Johnson, Ernest Dowson, John Davidson, Richard Le Gallienne, T. W. Rolleston, Edwin Ellis, John Todhunter, Arthur Symons, and other poets of Yeats's generation. There he could talk poetry to his peers, or, full of race and vision, dream of the awakening of Ireland and the part he was to play in it.

Subordinate to all these interests, when it is not a part of them, is Yeats's passion for Irish letters, his insistence that the proper subject for Irishmen is Ireland. There are many iterations of this belief in these letters, all of which are summarized for us in a brief sentence in A Ballad Singer: "With Irish literature and Irish thought alone have I to do." That is the banner under which Yeats charges, and he has been faithful to it in his fashion: only very occasionally does he allow himself to forget it. Browning dies, and Yeats comments on the relation of his optimism to his thought; the Rhymers' Club publishes, and Yeats devotes a letter in The Pilot to a discussion of the work of some of its members; there is a sale of autographs at Sotheby's, and apropos of that he writes of Blake and what is to him the most beautiful of his letters, one of the last Blake wrote, which contains a passage about the imagination that Yeats has never tired of quoting. But for the most part he sticks close to his last, and the result for us to-day is a body of contemporary comment which takes us behind the scenes of the Irish Renaissance before the curtain has gone up, while the play is still in rehearsal. The articles here rescued from the limbo of newspaper files allow us to see into the mind of the young poet when he is restlessly feeling his way to the ideas that are not only to determine the course of his own work, important as that is to be, but are also to prove of historical importance. The ideas that we find in these letters are to mould a movement, one of the most distinctive in the stream of English letters; brought forth by an unknown young Irish poet in London and printed in New England, they are part of a nation's awakening to intellectual and imaginative energy.

When we scan the ideas that Yeats expressed in these newspaper articles, we see that they all have their roots in five major beliefs. Yeats believed that an Irish writer should be national, should write of Irish life, and take it seriously. He was determined that the treasury of early Irish legend and folk-lore should be unlocked by translation, collection, and publication for Irish reader and writer alike. He realized that Irish poetry needed much discipline; that it must be purged of politics. He sensed that in the study of the occult, man might surprise the secret that would free him from the despotism of unhappiness. He hoped that after Ireland had an imaginative literature, she would be ripe for a national theatre.

II

Yeats testifies in one of his articles in The Pilot that it was his friendship with John O'Leary that awakened national feelings within him: "We of the younger generation owe a great deal to Mr. John O'Leary and his sister. What nationality is in the present literary movement in Ireland is largely owing to their influence — an influence all feel who come across them." It was the influence of John O'Leary that turned Yeats's imagination away from the Swedish princesses, Greek islands, Moorish magicians, Spanish Inquisitors, Hungarian patriots, and Indian scenes of the very early poems, in which Yeats's love of the far-away found expression, to Ireland's national legend and folk-lore. From his fine library of Irish books O'Leary lent Yeats the poems of Mangan, Ferguson, and Davis, and set him reading the other Irish poets who had written in English. It was owing to O'Leary that Yeats could write in The Pilot, "I know our Irish poets pretty thoroughly." It was O'Leary who made possible the publication of *The Wanderings of Oisin*; it was O'Leary, "the irreproachable patriot," who made the Irish Literary Society politically respectable among the Irish people generally; it was through O'Leary, indeed, as we have seen, that Yeats came to write for The Pilot the articles whose matter we are discussing. Yeats and Irish letters are much in debt to the fine old Fenian.

And not only has Yeats decided that Irish legend was to be the matter of his own verse, as *The Wanderings of Oisin* testifies, but he would have all Irishmen write of Irish themes. Irish writers whose subject matter is not Irish are condemned and sentenced to obscurity. Rolleston, who had birched Yeats in his review of *Oisin*, and who, having just translated Whitman into German, was now busy on a life of Lessing, calls forth from Yeats this sentence: "I wish he would devote his imagination to some national purpose." Remarks like "There is no fine literature without nationality" are frequent in these letters: "Allingham had the making of a great writer in him, but lacked impulse and momentum, the very things national feeling could have supplied. Whenever an Irish writer has strayed away from Irish themes and Irish feeling, in almost all cases he has done no more than make alms for oblivion." So John Francis O'Donnell and Miss Frances Wynne both belong to the same school of Irish writers. Instead

of steeping themselves in their own national life they "have read much English
literature, and have taken from it, rather
than from their own minds and the traditions of their own country, the manner
and matter of their poetry." So, too, of the
newly founded Irish Monthly Illustrated
Journal—"an Irish magazine should give
us Irish subjects."

So the song goes on with all the repeti-
tion of the passionate messiah. It is the
same song Yeats is to chant to Synge in
1896 in the rue d'Arras, sending Synge
away from Paris and his criticism of
French literature back to Ireland and the
writing of a drama so national that it is
understood by the Russian peasant.

It is a vision the truth of which is at-
tested by the sterility that seems to fall on
the transplanted Irish in our own day.
Both James Stephens and Sean O'Casey,
to take two of the preëminent Irish men
of letters of the generation that has succeeded Yeats, have left Ireland, and both
have produced little since they left Irish
soil and expressed the influences that
came to them there. Indeed the cosmo-

politanism that Yeats regrets in these articles has lost Irish literature, past and present, much: Irishmen have not only fought, they have written, for other nations; but to lose her men is one of the inevitable tragedies of an unsuccessful country.

The nationalism that the young Yeats had learned at the feet of John O'Leary in his house in Drumcondra, however, was not the political passion that had enslaved the energy of Ireland for hundreds of years. It was not the melodramatization of Ireland's past wrongs, with Ireland the fair heroine and England the dark villain, and all Irish literature one furious hiss. O'Leary was a critical nationalist. He had suffered imprisonment and exile from Ireland, but he could and did say such things as "There are things a man must not do to save a nation." Yeats's nationalism was critical and positive. It was designed not to spit at the Saxon villain but to recover the folk-lore and legend, that rich repository of Irish nationalism which Irishmen had allowed to lie so long neglected. It was out of the seed of this folk-

lore and legend that a new literature was
to spring.

III

A nation's legend and folk-lore are among
its most precious national treasures, and
Yeats desired ardently that these Irish
treasures should be collected and collected
well. And these were the years of their
gathering. He himself had edited a collection of Irish fairy and folk-tales in 1888,
and he was to do another volume in 1892.
In these two books he had selected what
interested him in the collections of Croker,
Lady Wilde, and Joyce, adding to them
stories he had taken out of the Irish novels
of Carleton, Lover, and Griffin, with one
or two stories collected by himself. Later,
in *The Celtic Twilight*, he was to give us a
volume of stories all of his own finding.
He had done much reading in the Irish
folk-tales for his editing, and so he came
well armed to the reviewing of new collections for The Journal and The Pilot.

In his review of McAnally's *Irish Wonders*, Yeats complains of the lack of seriousness of McAnally and his predecessors

in setting down the stories of the Irish people. He asks the question, "When will Irishmen record their legends as faithfully and seriously as Campbell did those of the Western Highlands?" Then he goes on to discuss McAnally's book in some detail, pointing out that McAnally "is wrong in saying that the Banshee never follows Irish families abroad," lamenting that McAnally fails to give the place and time of his recordings, but complimenting his phrasing, if not his pronunciations, and pleased that, unlike Croker and his school, he does not rationalize. Two or three times, to illustrate a point, Yeats tells stories of his own harvesting. One of these, how the ghost of a woman of Howth appeared to a neighbor woman to demand that her children be removed from the workhouse, Yeats tells again with greater fullness in *The Celtic Twilight*. Another story he has not, so far as I know, retold. Behind it lies what some one has called "the crookedness of the Gaelic mind."

A man at Ballysodare, a Sligo village not far from Coloonev, said once to me: "The stable boy up at Mrs. G——'s there met the master going round

the yards after he had been two days dead, and
told him to be away with him to the lighthouse,
and haunt that; and there he is far out to sea still,
sir. Mrs. G—— was that mad about it she dismissed the boy."

Six months later Yeats notes the forthcoming appearance of Jeremiah Curtin's
Irish Myths and Folk-Lore, some of whose
advance sheets Little, Brown and Company had sent him from Boston. Of this
Yeats expects much. In Curtin's introduction he finds as much science as he had
in Campbell and more imagination; his
book "promises to be the most careful
and scientific work on Irish folk-lore yet
published." Yeats promises a full review
of this book in The Pilot, but if he ever
sent this in, I have not been able to find it.

In the same letter in which Yeats mentions Curtin, he glances at Lady Wilde's
second book of Irish folk-lore, *Ancient
Cures, Charms, and Usages of Ireland*. He
has as yet had time to do no more than
turn the pages of the proverbs at the end.
Some of these he quotes, and we can see
one of them, "The lake is not encumbered
by its swan; nor the steed by its bridle;

nor the sheep by its wool; nor the man by
the soul that is in him," sinking into his
memory to be murmured over and over
again, as it is his habit to caress and fondle
phrases that please his mind and ear. He
quotes this proverb in the introduction to
his own *Irish Fairy Tales*, dropping out
the weakest of the four phrases, "nor the
sheep by its wool," so that the quotation
there has the symmetry of an Irish triad.

Hyde's *Beside the Fire* followed close
on the heels of these collections by Lady
Wilde and Curtin, and Yeats speaks highly
of this book in The Pilot. In Hyde Yeats
finds the folk-lorist he has been looking
for, one whose science, learning, imagination, and style answer the question he
asked in his review of McAnally's *Irish
Wonders:* "If Dr. Hyde carries out his
intentions, and continues to gather and
write out, in that perfect style of his, traditions, legends and old rhymes, he will give
the world one of those monumental works
whose absence from modern Irish literature I have been lamenting."

Hyde was to collect *The Songs of Connacht* and little more, alas; and although

he was to found in the Gaelic League a movement whose importance it is difficult to exaggerate, Ireland still lacks her monumental collection of Irish folk-lore.

To any one at all familiar with Irish letters the "accomplished Irish scholar, who is also perhaps the best Irish folklorist living," upon whom Yeats calls in his review, Irish Wonders, is no less clearly Hyde than is "a certain famous hedonist" who wrote "a letter on scented note paper" praising William Watson's Epigrams, Oscar Wilde. In these articles Hyde appears in a rôle which does him much honor — that of Scholar-in-Waiting to the Irish Renaissance. Yeats, Lady Gregory, and countless others have drawn again and again on the rich deposits of his scholarship, and his help was particularly valuable forty years ago when the Movement was just beginning and poor in scholarship. The notes with which he furnishes Yeats on the Irish word *fearsidh* and the anonymous song Shule Aroon are only two of hundreds which owe their existence to Hyde's generous response to a call for help from some swimmer struggling in the diffi-

cult depths of the Irish language and literature.

Yeats, however, did more than read and
edit Irish folk-lore, and preach the need of
getting it and Irish legend translated and
collected: he practiced what he preached;
he himself story-hunted among the Irish
peasants, and these stories so collected
are, and have remained, precious imaginative possessions. To-day in his Norman
tower, Thoor Ballylee, Yeats dreams over
stories he collected and imagined when
he was writing for The Journal and The
Pilot; he remembers Red Hanrahan, and
Mary Hynes, a peasant girl made famous
by Blind Raffery's song, and the "wild old
man in flannel" who could change a pack
of cards into a hare and a pack of hounds
that panted after it. Indeed this sensitiveness to folk-lore, this gift for remembering
with pleasure what men to-day no longer
care to remember, and making others
feel its charm, is one of the primary characteristics of most of Yeats's work, early
and late.

It was to this story-hunting, about
which Yeats speaks in A Ballad Singer,

that we are indebted for the legends set
down in *The Celtic Twilight*, a book he
wrote, as he tells Ashe King in the dedi-
cation to the *Early Poems and Stories*,
"when we were founding the National
Literary Society." In The Three O'Byrnes
we have the first printed version of the
story of that name in *The Celtic Twilight*,
one of those old stories about the evil of
buried treasure that we find in *Beowulf*
and all old folk literature.

Yeats's review in The Journal of Dr.
Todhunter's *The Banshee and Other Poems*
allows us to see the imaginative value that
Old Irish legend possessed for Yeats in
these years. Writing of the Mythological
Cycle of Old Irish romance, Yeats says:

His legends belong to those mythic and haunted
ages of the Tuatha De Danaan that preceded the
heroic cycle, ages full of mystery, where demons
and gods battle in the twilight. Between us and
them Cuchulain, Conall Carnach, Conary, Ferdiad and the heroes move as before gloomy arras.

In those mysterious pre-human ages when life
lasted for hundreds of years; when the monstrous
race of the Fomorians, with one foot, and one arm
in the middle of their chests, rushed in their pirate
galleys century after century like clouds upon the
coast; when a race of beautiful beings, whose living

hair moved with their changing thoughts, paced about the land; when the huge bulk of Balor had to be raised in his chariot, and his eyelid, weighted by the lassitude of age, uplifted with hooks that he might strike dead his foe with a glance — to these ages belongs the main portion of one legend supreme in innocence and beauty and tenderness, the tale of The Children of Lir.

"Whose living hair moved with their changing thoughts" is as beautiful in image and rhythm as anything in *Oisin*. Indeed, written early in 1889, the whole passage is in the mood of that poem, a *Götterdämmerung* such as that into which rode Niam and Oisin, and

    . . . Car-borne Balor, as old as a forest, his vast face sunk
    Helpless, men lifting the lids of his weary and death-pouring eye,

moved by Oisin in his dream.

There is little more of the matter of Old Irish legends in Yeats's articles. It is not that he was not thinking of them: they were as much in his mind as the folk-tales, as *The Wanderings of Oisin* proves, and the references to Goll, Fergus, Conchobar, Cuchulain, Emer, Diarmuid and Grania, Deirdre, and the Sons of Usna in the

poems from *Oisin* and *The Countess Cathleen*. That Irish history and legend were
even more important as matter for the
new Irish literature-to-be is stressed in
several of the letters. Between the man
of letters and Old Irish legend lay the
barrier of a very archaic, difficult, and
complicated language. Irish legend had
to wait, in the main, for the scholarship
that was to follow, as it always does, the
creative energy that made the Movement.

IV

What specific use and service Yeats
thought the recovery of this national legend and folk-lore would be to a modern
Anglo-Irish literature is made clear in a
long passage from Ireland's Heroic Age,
beginning:

The first thing needful if an Irish literature more
elaborate and intense than our fine but primitive
ballads and novels is to come into being is that
readers and writers alike should really know the
imaginative periods of Irish history.

Add to the thought of this passage two
sentences from the Irish National Literary
Society, where, speaking of books such as

Hyde's translations of the bardic tales, Yeats says:

It is impossible to overrate the importance of such books, for in them the Irish poets of the future will in all likelihood find a good portion of their subject matter. From that great candle of the past we must all light our little tapers.

These remarks tell us what part the recovery of this legend is to play in Yeats's program for a more "elaborate and intense" modern Anglo-Irish poetry. Yeats felt that the recovery in publication of this epic and folk literature would do for modern Anglo-Irish poetry what the publication of the old English ballads did for eighteenth century English poetry — rescue it from artificiality and bombast, give it substance and subtlety.

And not only must Irish poetry have this background of national epic and folk literature, it must no longer be the handmaid of Irish politics. Since the time of Swift, who on Irish soil first used poetry for political purposes, every strong political movement of the past hundred years, notably those of '98 and '48, had had its poets, and these poets had made a tradition in which the test of a poem was not the truth of its emotion, national or personal, but its patriotic or political hyperbole. This tradition was so deeply ingrained in Ireland as to be almost part of the national character, and Yeats encountered resistance here as he did elsewhere whenever he tried to engender a more critical spirit. Irishmen had made a goddess of Ireland, as the men of the Middle Ages developed the cult of the Virgin, calling Ireland Cathleen ni Houlihan, Dark Rosaleen, and other names of endearment; and poetry, like everything else, was to be her slave. Yeats worshipped at other shrines. The Intellectual Beauty, The Secret Rose, were the names which he and Shelley had imagined for their goddess, and nationalism was to serve her, and by so doing glorify itself. If we look deep into Yeats's mind, we see that for him nationalism was precious not so much because it served Ireland as because it well served Art. Ireland came not before, but after, Art.

Hand in hand with this insistence that Irish poetry be truly national and critical

went an inevitable revaluation of the
poets of the preceding generation. Just as
to-day in their own Renaissance the young
Scotch poets, led by Hugh M'Diarmid,
are setting Dunbar at the head of the
Scotch poets in the place of Burns, so
Yeats and his school were putting Mangan and Ferguson into the places formerly
held by Moore and Davis. And in these
articles it is being done under our eyes.
Ferguson, not Mangan, is the touchstone
Yeats uses to test the purity of an Irish
poet's nationalism; "the poems of Ferguson, Davis, and Mangan," a frequent
phrase, is undoubtedly a graded series.
When Yeats is writing these articles, Ferguson has passed Davis; it is later that
Mangan is elevated above both Davis and
Ferguson and placed at the head of the
poets of Young Ireland.

In Yeats's review of William Allingham's *Irish Songs and Poems*, the first
poet of the new order passes judgment on
the last poet of the old, and the verdict is:
"These poems are not national." Like
McAnally, Allingham does not take the
Irish people seriously; to him they and

their life are but "a half serious memory."
But here the young critic pays for his
principles, for the memories are beautiful,
and when Allingham writes of his native
Ballyshannon, Yeats remembers Sligo, and
the pull of sentiment against principle
is strong. When, however, Yeats measures Allingham against Davis and Ferguson, Allingham's lack of nationalism
becomes too evident to be ignored.

In his review of Todhunter's *The Banshee*, Yeats again sets nationalism against
cosmopolitanism, as he had in writing of
Allingham; and again Ferguson is the
measuring rod of the nationalism of the
poet on trial. This time the verdict is for
the poet reviewed: "Dr. Todhunter no
longer comes to us as an art poet: he
claims recognition as one of the national
writers of the Irish race." He has done
what his fellow exile failed to do — re-
sponded to the newly awakened national
tradition. A younger man than Allingham, he was able to react to forces that
were dominating men twenty years his
junior. Three years later Yeats notices in
The Pilot a shilling reprint of *The Ban-*

shee, summarizing his long Journal review in a sentence: "Dr. Todhunter follows in the footsteps of Sir Samuel Ferguson and gives us simple and stately versions of The Children of Lir and Sons of Turann."

In Yeats's first note in The Pilot on Miss Ellen O'Leary's poems he writes: "Miss O'Leary's poems . . . are the last notes of that movement of song, now giving place to something new, that came into existence when Davis, singing, rocked the cradle of a new Ireland." In these words Yeats summarizes fifty years of Anglo-Irish poetry, from the rhetorical vehemence of Davis and other poets of The Nation, through the quiet simplicity of the Fenians, Kickham, Casey, and Miss O'Leary, to the "something new" that stood affirmed in *Poems and Ballads of Young Ireland*. And he is quite conscious that he stands between the waning of one burst of energy and the waxing of another.

The death of Miss O'Leary moved Yeats: her going stood as a sign of the passing of a generation to whose moral grandeur and nobility of character he has paid tribute in his poem with the refrain,

"It's with O'Leary in the grave." Yeats had announced Miss O'Leary's forthcoming volume of poems in The Pilot for August 3, 1889, praising the Wordsworthian simplicity of her best poems. Two years later when her posthumous book, *Lays of Country, Home and Friends*, finally appeared, he writes of her again, selecting for praise To God and Ireland True, "a song in the old sense of the word, that is to say, a singable poem worthy of good music. The compilers of our songbooks, ballad sheets and the like, should garner it." Yeats took his own advice to heart, for eight years later he put it into his *Book of Irish Verse*.

There are also notes on a group of young women who, in the sociable manner of the Irish, gathered around the fireside of The Irish Monthly, as the poets of The Nation surrounded their paper, and the Fenian poets John O'Leary's journal, The Irish People. A Miss Ryan, who published *Songs of Remembrance* in 1889 and then passed into obscurity, is dismissed with the succinct comment, "She is too sad by a great deal." I have already quoted what

Yeats said of Miss Wynne's verses — they were not national, though Yeats is quite conscious that in this case such criticism is, as he says, a little like breaking a butterfly on a wheel. To Rose Kavanagh, who also like Miss Wynne died young, Yeats devotes a whole article. In her much promise was first dimmed by bad health and then soon quenched by death. Yeats compares her to Kickham and Casey. She left two or three poems that have survived in all but the most recent of Irish anthologies. And Miss Tynan, the best known and most prolific of all the young women of this group, Yeats praises perfunctorily, more in gratitude and friendship, it seems to me, than in desire.

These notes are all Yeats has to say of the poetry of his Irish contemporaries. In writing of them, he is either gently critical or faint in praise, and this is as it should be, but, like Percy, his blood beats to a ballad which he buys from a ballad singer in the County Down, with the refrain, "Where the ancient shamrocks grow," of which he quotes three stanzas. I find it pretty commonplace, but then I read in 1933, I do not hear in 1891. The young Yeats is exclamatorily extravagant in its praise: "What infinite sadness there is in these verses! What wild beauty!"

In his Pilot letter for April 23, 1892, Yeats writes of the Rhymers' Club, its members, and their poetry. Notable as are many of these names to-day, when Yeats writes of them they are, like him, unknown, just beginning their work. For mention he selects Arthur Symons, whom he describes as "a scholar in music halls as another man might be a Greek scholar or an authority on the age of Chaucer." Symons, Yeats contrasts with John Davidson, who has also selected the music halls for his material. In both these young men Yeats finds the search for new matter that was as characteristic of the Rhymers as was the search for new forms of the generation of poets just passing. And from what Yeats says here of their wistfulness for their lost Philistinism, it would seem that by 1892, three years before Wilde reached the height of his fame and power, the young Rhymer was already weary of aestheticism, "an Alastor tired of his woods and longing for beer and skittles."

Like Italy in her Renaissance, Ireland in the years when she was discovering her age was alive with the stirrings of her youth: it is not for nothing that Yeats's Cathleen ni Houlihan is both an old woman and a glimmering girl. Passages like the one with which Yeats concludes his notes on the Rhymers are frequent in these letters: "England is old and her poets must scrape up the crumbs of an almost finished banquet, but Ireland has still full tables." It was this same consciousness of Ireland's youth and England's age that in 1899 decided George Moore to answer his echo-augury, "Go to Ireland." No Irish man of letters, least of all Moore, could listen unmoved and unexcited to sentences such as the one at the end of Yeats's letter on The Irish National Literary Society: "If we can but put those tumultuous centuries into tale or drama, the whole world will listen to us and sit at our feet like children who hear a new story." In such remarks lie the seed of Yeats and Moore's *Diarmuid and Gra-*

nia, and much of the Anglo-Irish literature that has followed it.

Of the work of William Watson, who
joined the Rhymers but never came to
their meetings, Yeats writes at length in
The Journal. With the young man's love
of strong antitheses he divides the writers
of verse into "the poets who rouse and
trouble, the poets who hush and console," and then places Watson among the
latter.

In this review we have an early affirma-
tion of Yeats's love of "an extravagant,
exuberant, mystical" art, which was undoubtedly fostered in him by his father's
admiration of intensity. Yeats admires
much the art of Watson's verses and pays
them the tribute of committing them to
memory, but this poetry is too much in
the Matthew Arnold tradition to be admired with both the head and the heart by
one who had wandered spiritually hand in
hand with Ellis down Blake's pathway of
excess. Yeats writes of Watson's poems
with all the condescension that those
who have intensity feel for those who
have it not.

But while at this time Yeats admired the art of William Watson, he was not to know him as well as some of the others. Of the Rhymers, Yeats was to know best Davidson, Johnson, and Symons. From the first two he ultimately drifted away because of the irritability bred of frustration in the one, and the great appetite for drink in the other that turned sociability with him into pity and sorrow. Symons, however, became his intimate and influenced his art. Symons had what Yeats lacked at this time, art and scholarship, and Yeats himself has testified how much his theory and practice were influenced by what Symons read him from Catullus, Verlaine, and Mallarmé, in particular how much the elaborate form of some of the poems in *The Wind Among the Reeds* owes to Symons's translations of Mallarmé.

For among the Rhymers Yeats was forming his style. If we look for a moment at the two poems Yeats contributed to The Pilot and The Journal, we can see in what need Yeats stood of criticism in these years. The first of these, How Ferencz Renyi Kept Silent, describes a dramatic

moment in which a Hungarian patriot is
tortured for information by an Austrian
general. His mother, sister, and sweetheart are shot successively in an effort
to make him reveal the whereabouts of
his countrymen. After the shooting of
the sweetheart, Ferencz goes insane and
rushes away "rolling from his lips a mad-
man's laugh." In this poem, obviously
an imitation of Browning's dramatic dia-
logues which succeeds only in being melo-
dramatic, all is thin, surface violence, fire
without heat or light. The second poem,
The Phantom Ship, is equally violent,
though it has more academic interest for
us, for we can see in it how the poet was
beginning to use Irish folk-lore for the
matter of his poems. In Irish Wonders
Yeats tells us, "One old man in County
Sligo told me a story of a man who saw all
who had died out of his village for years,
sitting in a fairy rath one night." Make
the village a fishing village, and change
the fairy rath to a phantom ship craz-
ily riding a squall, while all those ever
drowned from that village stand grey and
silent under a sky dizzy with lightning,

and you have The Phantom Ship. But the Irish quality of the legend is hidden under anonymity: there is nothing more definite than "a pale priest" to suggest that the scene of this poem is an Irish village. And technically the poems are poor; energetic rhythms in iambic pentameter and trochaic octameter, both rhymed with such rhymes as *wine* and the *shine* that is contracted *sunshine*, fall strangely on ears that know only Yeats's later verses.

So much of what has come to be Yeats's poetic ethic is here in these articles, either directly or by clear inference, that it is surprising not to find the hatred of rhetoric which for years so dominated Yeats's judgment that, as he has remarked to me, "I then thought much rhetorical that I should now think otherwise." Certainly if he had developed this scorn for rhetoric by 1890, the admiration for Victor Hugo's *Shakespeare* with which he begins his review of William Watson's poems, to say nothing of "the poets who rouse and trouble, the poets who hush and console," which is pure Swinburne in both rhetoric

and rhythm, are very strange. It must
have come later.

V

One of the most fascinating folds in
Yeats's mind is his love of symbol, mysticism, magic, clairvoyance, hypnotism,
cabalistic science — all the occult means
by which men seek the Infinite through
a study of what seem to them its mani-
festations. As a young man, fresh from
the gentle agnostic influence of his father,
John Butler Yeats, Yeats had made himself a little private religion out of the fables of old stories and notable personages
from history and literature, really a poet's
culture held with the passion of a religious
belief. With this as a center of belief he
turned successively to the study of Oriental pantheism through theosophy, to the
worship of Shelley's Intellectual Beauty,
to the passionate mysticism of Blake's
Prophetical Books, to modern Cabalism,
to the symbolism of the French Decadents, finally to the astronomical psychol-
ogy of his recent *A Vision*, all of which
have ministered to the imaginative intel-

lectualism which is the passion of his life.
And he has approached them all, not as a
true mystic but in the mood in which one
says, "Yes, I believe in ghosts and fairies." He has believed in these doctrines
emotionally, not intellectually, as one believes emotionally, not rationally, in the
ghost of Hamlet's father, or as some men
of agnostic tendencies believe in God. He
has sampled all the imaginative stimulants from table-rapping to Shelley's Intellectual Beauty, and they have been to
him what other stimulants have been to
other poets. To trace their succession by
means of the marks they have left upon
his poetry and prose will be the passion of
some future scholar in poetry. Now we
are attentive to the traces they have left
here in these early articles.

In one of his first letters to The Pilot
Yeats mentions Colonel Olcott's lectures
in Dublin on Irish goblins. Colonel Olcott, the American president of the Theo-
sophical Society, was something of an
expert on ghosts, goblins, and phantoms;
he had, among other studies, translated
and annotated Adolphe D'Assier's *Essai*

sur l'humanité posthume et le spiritisme, and he had also the gift of persuasion. Says Yeats of Colonel Olcott's lectures in Dublin:

He asserted that such things really exist, and so strangely has our modern world swung back on its old belief, so far has the reaction from modern materialism gone, that his audience seemed rather to agree with him. He returns to London at once, where the faithful of his creed are busy with many strange schemes — among the rest the establishing of an occult monastery in Switzerland, where all devout students of the arcane sciences may bury themselves from the world for a time or forever.

Yeats also tells the readers of The Pilot that Madame Blavatsky, "the pythoness of the Movement, holds nightly levees at Lansdowne Road." It is difficult to judge from what Yeats has written about this woman just how seriously he took her and her doctrine. Not very seriously, I am sure: one does not call the high priestess of a belief one reverences, a pythoness. Yeats went to Lansdowne Road to listen to Madame Blavatsky because "her imagination contained all the folk-lore of the world." Her belief that there was another globe stuck on the earth at the North

Pole, that the shape of the earth was really a dumb-bell — this belief and others like it excited Yeats's imagination. For the same reason he took long walks with Æ in Ireland when Æ was unintelligible with the vision that was in him, "for the sake of some stray sentence, beautiful and profound, amid many words that seemed without meaning." So he read the imaginative algebra of the Cabala, so he studied Blake's symbolical writings, so he sat at the seances of the Hermetic Students. When in these years Yeats wrote to Katharine Tynan of Æ's mysticism: "You must not blame him for that. It gives originality to his pictures and his thoughts," he might well have been apologizing for himself. By these toyings and dabblings around the edges of magic and theosophy and mysticism, Yeats loosened his imagination, thickening the cloud of dreams about him out of which he was to summon the images of his poetry.

Yeats speaks also in The Pilot of his study of the Cabala. In a review of Dr. Todhunter's little play, *The Poison Flower*, he writes, "The copy of the Kabala that lies upon my own desk pleads for him, and tells us that such men lived, and may well have dreamed just such a dream, in the mystic Middle Ages." The malicious Moore has questioned whether Yeats did any more than allow the Cabala to lie upon his desk, but when Moore doubted, Yeats had not yet written *A Vision*. If Moore read that, he no longer could have doubted. The mind that could write *A Vision* could read the Cabala, easily.

I have previously mentioned Yeats's friendship with MacGregor Mathers; it was he who introduced Yeats to the Hermetic Students; it was he, the author of *The Kabbalah Unveiled*, I am sure, who interested Yeats in the Cabala, a book whose form Yeats certainly remembered when, forty years later, he wrote *A Vision*. It was Mather who set the great poet of our generation trying to excite a cat by imagining a mouse in front of its nose, but a man of genius must do something, I suppose, to rid himself of the imaginative turbulence within him, and who dares say where imagination ends and magic begins. Many a thing that in the doing seems foolish yields results at which only a fool can smile.

The interest in Blake that stands revealed in the Ellis and Yeats edition of that mystic is recorded in another early article in The Pilot. Here Yeats quotes a passage from one of Blake's letters, a letter sold at Sotheby's for eight pounds, ten shillings:

I have been very near the gates of death, and have returned very weak, and an old man feeble and tottering, but not in spirits and life, not in the real man, the imagination which liveth forever. In that I am stronger and stronger as this foolish body decays. . . . Flaxman is gone, and we must all soon follow, everyone to his own eternal house.

One wonders how much of this passage Yeats remembered when, forty years later, he calls out in The Tower:

What shall I do with this absurdity —
O heart, O troubled heart — this caricature,
Decrepit age that has been tied to me
As to a dog's tail?
             Never had I more
Excited, passionate, fantastical
Imagination!

Out of all this preoccupation with the occult and the mystical has emerged one belief which I fancy means something to Yeats and his poetry. Out of his association with Æ and Oriental thought, out of his reading of Shelley and Blake, out of his fellowship with the Theosophists and the Hermetic Students came somehow the belief that every personal imagination is part of the Divine Mind. And every personal imagination, therefore, because it is part of that Divine Mind, can, in favorable moments, receive intuitions of what men, also with a share in that Mind, have felt before it. It is this belief which moves Yeats to say, "People do not invent, they remember"; where to remember is to speak with the voice of the Divine Mind. It is these studies and experiences that prompt Yeats to write, when he himself sums up what he drew from them, "Images well up before the mind's eye from a deeper source than conscious or subconscious memory." A great audacious metaphor, in other words, is a glimpse into a divine order: he who wrote "The spirit of man is the candle of the Lord," saw God. It is this belief which causes Yeats to see in folk-lore and legend a body of metaphor under which may be revealed to men to-day the mind and soul of the past. So in Browning Yeats writes:

To the old folk-lorists, fables and fairy tales were a haystack of dead follies, wherein the virtuous might find one little needle of historical truth. Since then Joubainville and Rhys and many more have made us see in all these things old beautiful mythologies wherein ancient man said symbolically all he knew about God and man's soul, once famous religions fallen into ruin and turned into old wives' tales, but still luminous from the rosy dawn of human revery.

This is why symbol, whether that symbol be Deirdre or her story, is so precious: it carries the imagination back to all that lies behind it; through it men may recover forgotten truths and unremembered beauty.

VI

"A man's life of any worth is a continual allegory," said Keats, and perhaps in that remark lies the clue to the spectacle of a man who has made it his life's work to evolve a lonely, distant, indirect, aristocratic art, spending ten or more years of his life in the hurly-burly of organization

and propaganda. That Yeats was not un-
conscious of this contradiction of ideal and
practice, we have ample evidence. In a
letter to Lady Gregory written in 1901 in
the midst of the turmoil of the rehearsals
of *Diarmuid and Grania*, Yeats says, "I
might have been away, away in the country, in Italy perhaps, writing poems for
my equals." And once when I spoke to
him of it, he said, "It has bothered my
conscience." But confession or no confession, we must always remember that
every Irishman is a born propagandist,
and incorrigible. Has not Yeats only recently organized the Irish Academy and
toured America to collect funds for it?

Yeats's review of the poems of John
Francis O'Donnell brings us into touch
with the Southwark Irish Literary Club
and the beginning of the ten years of organization and propaganda. This club,
founded in 1883 to take care of the Irish
children in South London, had become
literary. Yeats had lectured there on
Sligo fairies, and the club had collected
and published the works of Irish poets,
among them O'Donnell's poems. Yeats

cared little for O'Donnell's verses, but he saw in the Southwark Literary Club, which was ceasing to function, the nucleus for a society that might do for Irish letters what the Rhymers' Club was doing for the young British poets in London. Accordingly in 1891 he invited the Committee to meet at his father's house in Bedford Square, and out of that meeting grew The Irish Literary Society. Yeats induced Rolleston and his father-in-law, Stopford Brooke, and others to throw themselves into its work, and the society was joined by most of the Irish authors and journalists then living in London.

A few months later Yeats is in Ireland founding there The Irish National Literary Society, "and affiliating it with certain Young Ireland Societies in country towns which seemed anxious to accept its leadership." He is writing from the new National Library, and, no doubt remembering his father's injunction never to study anything with a practical end in view, he is dismayed by the sight of readers for only what may be turned into pounds and shillings. And then, in this last letter to The Pilot, he calls upon his countrymen to unite literature to their great political passion, to read the literature of their nation which the new Library of Ireland is to bring them, to live as the men of '48 lived, "by the light of noble books and the great traditions of the past."

In this plea Yeats comes dangerously near ideals. Had his father read this, he would have said, "Take care, Willie; ideals thin the blood and take the human nature out of people." But devotion to the cause of Art, not purpose to improve Irish character, is the real motive behind his words here. The political propagandists of the preceding decades of the nineteenth century had made literature the servant of politics. Yeats would reverse that relation, making nationalism the handmaid of Art. He would woo the Irish to an interest in their literature by appealing to their love of Dark Rosaleen. The improvement in the national character that might result from this revived interest in literature is secondary to the call to a disinterested intellectualism.

The disgust of Irishmen with public affairs of which Yeats speaks in this passage:

So far all has gone well with us, for men who are saddened and disgusted with the turn public affairs have taken have sought in our society occasion to do work for Ireland that will bring about assured good,

is a reference to the wave of revolt and self-nausea that swept over Ireland when the Irish people realized that they had allowed their leaders to persuade them to betray Parnell, a mental attitude which, as Yeats points out, had made Ireland receptive to his ideas. Yeats's Movement was a return to the people in the sense that it was an appeal directly to the people, over the heads of the leaders who had misled them.

VII

Behind all these plans and interests — this cry to Irish writers to be national, this passionate desire to see Ireland's legends and folk-lore revived, rescued, and put into the consciousness of the Irish race, this purging of Irish poetry of politics, this interest in the occult, this propaganda and organization — behind all this is the dream of a national drama for Ireland. At this time it is not a working plan: Yeats does not immediately urge an Irish theatre as he does the translation of Old Irish legends and the publication of Irish books. It exists now as a dream of an ideal national theatre, to be turned over in the mind until such time as the foundations for it shall have been laid. Remembering these years, Yeats writes in *The Trembling of the Veil*, " I had definite plans; I wanted to create an Irish Theatre; I was finishing my *Countess Cathleen* in its first meagre version, and thought of a travelling company to visit our country branches; but before that there must be a popular imaginative literature." These plans are set down here in these two New England papers ten years before the actual beginnings of the Irish Dramatic Movement in 1899.

We find these plans stated in what Yeats wrote about the London performances of Dr. Todhunter's three plays, *Helena in Troas*, *A Sicilian Idyll*, and *The*

Poison Flower. Yeats was much interested in these plays and their performance, particularly in the *Idyll*, a poetical pastoral play, which he had persuaded Todhunter to write for performance in the little red brick theatre in Bedford Park. The play was a great success, and Yeats wrote of its triumph in both The Journal and The Pilot. The next year the play was put on at the Vaudeville, one of the big Strand theatres, and for this occasion Todhunter wrote to precede the *Idyll* another poetic play, *The Poison Flower*, founded on Hawthorne's Rappaccini's Daughter. Yeats also wrote of these performances for both papers.

George Moore has described Yeats's original idea of a theatre (he is writing of the Yeats of 1899) as "a little mist, some fairies, and a psaltery." That is very witty, and as true as raillery can ever be. Those were Yeats's foibles, and he knew as little as Ole Bull about the actual business of conducting a theatre: both were Don Quixotes charging the technical difficulties of theatrical enterprise, one with a fiddle bow, the other with a psaltery.

But although Yeats knew little of the technic of the stage, he was possessed of very definite ideas on the drama. He despised the contemporary theatre which imitates life for the many. What he wanted was a drama whose matter was to be the national legends, a drama revealing through stories that were old enough to have become symbolical, life that would stir men's imagination and move their emotions. This drama was to be a poetic one, and its model was the Elizabethan drama. Its speech, like that of the Elizabethans, was to be exuberant, vehement, fantastic, abundant. These plays were to be produced so as to accent the speaking of the verse, movement was to be stately and deliberate, scenery impressionistic; nothing was to be allowed to make for a restlessness that would interfere with the beautiful speaking of verse. Finally this drama was to be played before a small, select audience, who should come reverently to the play as if they were Catholics coming to Mass. Yeats's disgust with the commercial theatre of his day is the perennial one of the artist with a theatre that is always so much a lesser thing than he can imagine it to be. In Yeats's opinion the whole of the spoken drama has divorced itself from literature, and its falseness stings Yeats into many a contemptuous phrase. It is the old story of the young man of taste and talent, his mind full of the masterpieces of the past, in the presence of machine-made drama for the many.

Loving beautiful speech, Yeats desires a poetic drama, for which, naturally enough, his model is Elizabethan. He knows that the days when "everyone, from the pot boys to the noblemen, thought imagination a high and worthy thing" are gone, that England has become unimaginative, Puritan, and rich; but the reception of Dr. Todhunter's poetic plays causes him to believe that there is a small, perhaps growing, public for the poetic play, on which such a drama might be founded.

There is in Yeats great scorn, not only for the thought and action of contemporary drama, but for its language as well. There are many contemptuous ref-

erences to its speech of the street and the
tea table. Yeats desires the exuberant,
vehement speech of a drama in which the
hero when greatly moved does not merely
stare steadily and silently into an open
hearth but speaks the great poetical oratory of the Shakespearean soliloquy. As
yet, however, there is no thought that
the speech of the English-speaking, but
Gaelic-thinking, Irish peasant of the West
can supply that idiom. That is to come
later out of Yeats's friendship with Lady
Gregory.

It was a woman, also, who drew Yeats's
attention to the speaking of verse. Florence Farr, or Mrs. Edward Emery, to give
her her married name, played in both the
Idyll and *The Poison Flower*. She brought
to the speaking of Todhunter's lines a
monotonous chant-like recitation of verse
that gave to each syllable its full volume
of sound, and a rhythmic dreaminess of
movement and gesture for which Yeats
found it difficult to find high praise
enough. Heron Allen, another amateur —
indeed so much a one that he insisted upon
appearing on the program as Mr. Smith —

also pleased Yeats greatly. From that day
to this Yeats has believed that the cultivated man or woman makes the best per-
former of poetic plays, and Maude Gonne
in *Cathleen ni Houlihan* and Ezra Pound
in the London rehearsals of *The Hawk's
Well* have done much to bear him out.

It was with Miss Farr that Yeats began
his experiments of speaking verse to music in an effort to release poetry from its
slavery to music in song. Deaf to the
power of music, Yeats sees it when it is
combined with words in song or opera as
something that destroys the speech balance of consonant and vowel, distorts the
rhythms of words, and slows down the
speed of the transmission of thought. He
would go back to the time before "music
grew too proud to be the garment of
words," for music developed latest of all
the arts and in its early days was humble.
What Yeats desires is a musical recitation
of words, with little more music in the background than one hears in *recitativo secco*.

The remainder of Yeats's theory of production can easily be inferred if we remember that all the other elements in the

ensemble must, like music, be subordinate
to the verse. Movement is to be deliberate; gesture restrained and subtle; scenery
impressionistic, a vague background, stim-
ulating the imagination, not feeding the
eye with imitative detail; even costume
must be simple in form and color lest it
distract the attention of the audience from
the voice of the speaker.

The audience that Yeats sees in the pit
of his ideal theatre is not to come to the
theatre frivolously, chattering the gossip
of the street, but quietly, reverently, like
suppliants to an oracle of which the dramatist is the high priest. In The Children
of Lir he writes: "We must go to the stage
all eagerness like a mob of eavesdroppers
and to be inspired, not amused, if modern
drama is to be anything else than a muddy
torrent of shallow realism." In 1889
Yeats writes in a Providence paper, "We
must go to the stage all eagerness like a
mob of eavesdroppers"; in the winter of
1932 in a lecture at Wellesley, remembering better than he knew, he said: "I
wanted a theatre hard to get into, like a
secret society."

Yeats has been faithful to this conception of the drama. He has written plays for the reverent few. And his interest in the old Noh plays of Japan is anticipated here more than twenty-five years before their influence stirred him to invent a form of drama that answers in every detail this youthful dream.

But this meeting with Florence Farr did more than set Yeats theorizing over the details of dramatic production: she has influenced further his life and work. It was with her that he joined the Hermetic Students; it was her image that he saw and her voice that he heard when he was writing *The Countess Cathleen*, *Cathleen ni Houlihan*, and the early dramatic poems; it was for her that he wrote his *Land of Heart's Desire* in 1894, when she was manageress of the Avenue Theatre and needed a curtain-raiser for Shaw's *Arms and the Man*; it was with her that he thought, in 1898, remembering the small club theatre in Bedford Park, of taking a little theatre in the London suburbs for the production of romantic plays; it was she, as we have seen, who was responsible for the experiments in speaking verse to music; it was she, "the lady in the green cloak," whom Moore found at the rehearsals of *The Countess Cathleen* murmuring the line, "Cover it up with a lonely tune," to the accompaniment of the psaltery, while the experienced actress Moore had engaged strode to and fro like a pantheress. It is of her and her art that he has written in his essays and autobiographies; it is she upon whom he calls thirty years later, in All Souls' Night, when in a mood of grave ecstasy he feels the need of a mind freed from all earthly calls outside its own pondering:

On Florence Emery I call the next,
Who finding the first wrinkles on a face
Admired and beautiful,
And knowing that the future would be vexed
With 'minished beauty, multiplied commonplace,
Preferred to teach a school,
Away from neighbour or friend
Among dark skins, and there
Permit foul years to wear
Hidden from eyesight to the unnoticed end.

VIII

These articles also set us thinking about another beautiful woman who was to influence Yeats's life and his art even more than Florence Farr. Ever since the day Maude Gonne stepped out of her hansom cab in Bedford Park on one of her numerous journeys between Dublin and Paris, her beauty has haunted Yeats's imagination, exciting him to write the beautiful love poems in which he has sought for images to express her loveliness.

In The Pilot for July 30, 1892, Yeats reports a long speech Maude Gonne made at the Catholic University of Luxembourg, printed in the supplement to La Revue Catholique. This was one of the many speeches she was making in France on the story of Ireland's wrongs. Yeats tells us that thousands have come "to see this new wonder — a beautiful woman who makes speeches," that "at Bordeaux, an audience of twelve hundred persons rose to its feet, when she had finished, to applaud her with wild enthusiasm." He quotes her description of the famine of

1848, praising the beauty and power of her oratory.

In Maude Gonne was the energy that animated Young Ireland at this time. And she and her image have moulded many a line of the poet's verse. She is Yeats's Laura, and he who would understand much of Yeats's very allusive poetry must learn of her. Both she and Florence Farr scorned the great beauty that was in them, and Yeats has raged at both of them because of it. Florence Farr, neglecting also her gift of beautiful speech, turned to the study of the occult and finally ended her days teaching English to the natives of Ceylon. Maude Gonne, filled with a destroying energy, as Florence Farr was with a destroying curiosity, grew daily more shrill in argument, more violent in action, while Yeats looked on, furious that Demeter, banner in hand, should lead the Dublin lines that picketed the first performances of *The Plough and the Stars*. But, as Yeats himself has cried of her in No Second Troy,

> Why, what could she have done being what she is?
> Was there another Troy for her to burn?

IX

It is interesting to see, now that over forty years have passed since Yeats wrote the first of these letters to the New Island, how time has turned much of his intuition and logic into fact.

Irish writers have become national, have written out of the forces, ancient and modern, that have vivified and moulded Irish life, and have been, or will be, accepted by their countrymen accordingly.

The legends and folk literature for whose gathering, translation, and reading Yeats plead have been gathered, translated, and read. The books of Lady Gregory, Rolleston, and others have restored Irish legend; Cuchulain and Deirdre have been reborn. *The Tain* has been translated and published. Hyde has collected the songs of Connacht and the tales of inland Connacht; Larminie, the tales of the coast of Connacht and Donegal; Curtin, those of Munster. Scholars in Old Irish, notably Kuno Meyer, have edited and translated many of the Old Irish texts. These texts have been used by men of letters, remarkably by James Stephens.

Irish poetry has been put to school. It has lost its rhetoric and political passion, and become artistic. In beauty and subtlety of movement, in the cunning voweling which it inherits from the Gaelic bards of the seventeenth and eighteenth centuries, it to-day yields to no poetry in English. It has become "distinguished and lonely," notably in the poems of Yeats, Lionel Johnson, Seumas O'Sullivan, Padraic Colum, and James Stephens. The recent anthologies of Colum and Lennox Robinson will convince any critic of its fullness and its artistry. It still, however, lacks its epic masterpiece, but there have been few epic masterpieces in the poetry of any nation in the last hundred years.

Irish legend has provided the poets of modern Ireland with a body of symbol through which they have been able to express a personal emotion. Indeed in the last forty years Deirdre has grown so deeply into the world's imagination that she has almost as many lovers among men to-day as have Helen, Dido, Guinevere, to mention only her most famous rivals. And the stories of the Red Branch, which are her *Iliad*, are to-day as powerful an influence in Irish letters as the Arthurian Legend has been in English.

An Irish drama has been born. It has not developed exactly as Yeats planned it, for Dublin has not been made folk-minded and for the most part the plays it has looked upon at the Abbey have not been poetical plays based on the national legends. Yeats and Moore's *Diarmuid and Grania*, Æ's *Deirdre*, Synge's *Deirdre*, and a few small poetical pieces by Daniel Corkery and Austin Clarke are about all the poetical drama, or drama based on national legend, that the Abbey has seen, except the poetical plays of Yeats's own making. Yeats's program of legend and poetry for the drama was too narrow for a living theatre in these days. Synge's peasant plays and O'Casey's plays of the Dublin slum-dweller have been the notable work of this theatre, with many imitations of Synge, and so far no successful ones of O'Casey. Synge's plays, however, while they were not, except for *Deirdre*, based on national legends, or in verse, fulfilled Yeats's desire for "a fantastic, energetic, extravagant art," and O'Casey's speech excites like drink, sending a shock of joy to the blood. As yet the Irish middle classes have had little opportunity to see themselves on the stage of the Abbey, but so much the better for their peace of mind, one who knows Dublin has said, truthfully enough. However, that is the direction in which the Irish drama must spread; that is the highway as yet unbarred by genius that lies open for the coming Irish dramatist.

No man ever shaped a large movement exactly to a pre-arranged pattern, but I think what I have just said shows that Yeats has done almost that. And I come from the contemplation of these facts with a great admiration for the vision, energy of mind, tact, and wisdom of the man who has remade the literature of a nation. Anyone who knows Ireland, its poverty, its pride, and its passion, knows the enormous difficulties that beset Yeats, of which the disturbances over *The Countess*

Cathleen in 1899, *The Playboy* in 1907, *The Plough and the Stars* in 1926, are dramatic explosions, the growing-pains of the awakened Irish mind.

The work that Yeats accomplished could only be wrought by an intense energy, and intense energy and concentration are qualities upon which satire is sure to seize: ridicule is the tribute paid them by a lesser energy and a lesser dream. So Moore has snickered maliciously and O'Casey with all the violence of the sentimentalist has growled and snarled from his exile in London, muttering "The Great Founder" under his breath. But we are not deceived; put to the test, these two men would be the first to pay the tribute of praise as they have the tribute of satire.

It is impossible to read these letters without constantly looking forward, as I have done, to what has grown out of them. In their rapid words of the moment are most of the ideas that have shaped the work of the great Irish poet of our time, and much of the Movement with which his name is joined; and it is what the years have made of these ideas that

gives these letters their full meaning and
their appeal to the imagination. That is
their chief value. But they have still another interest. These early letters allow
us to see the young poet when he has just
emerged from boyhood, when fame has
not withered his freshness, when, simple
and eager, he is flushed with the ideas that
possess him, and writing, as Yeats himself
said when he read these letters again recently, better than he knew. The beautiful autobiographical *Four Years* contains
the thoughts of youth recollected in ma-
turity; they are the interest on the experiences of which these letters, which com-
plement them, are part of the capital.
Beside the reminiscent mood of the *Autobiographies*, the letters are pungent with
immediate, living comment; they permit
us to come closer than we can elsewhere to
a man of genius the undulating rhythms
of whose later, formal prose hold us at a
distance, so that even in so intimate a
form as autobiography, Yeats seems to
utter his sentences like a voice in Greek
tragedy, speaking unseen from within
some great temple.

F

While the style of these letters lacks the invariable high literary breeding of the later prose — not that the Yeatsian hall mark isn't here somewhere on every piece — they tell us many things for which we are grateful. They were written before Yeats's surrender to the fascination of the difficult, and in them is much of the revealing, accidental self.

FROM THE BOSTON PILOT

MR. WILLIAM WILLS

ENGLAND is an old nation, the dramatic fervor has perhaps ebbed out of her. However that may be, most of the best dramas on the English stage from the times of Congreve and Sheridan and Goldsmith to our own day have been the work of Irishmen. The most prominent London dramatist at the present time is certainly the Irishman, Mr. W. Wills; his much more renowned countryman, Mr. Dion Boucicault, can hardly any longer be called a London dramatist. The revival of Mr. Wills' *Claudian* at the Princess, previous to its departure for America, has brought up again the old gossip as to the disputed authorship of the famous earthquake incident which concludes the piece. As a matter of fact the whole merit of the originality belongs to Mr. Wills, and dates as far back as the year following the catastrophe at Ischia, when Mr. Wills, being in Rome, wrote the piece in communication with eye witnesses of the kind of incident he was venturing for the first time to introduce into a drama. But rumor would have it that he was a mere poet and incapable of so scenic a conception. His collaborator was also a man of literature and not equal to so great a stage climax. The manager had a brief period of glory, but then it was decided that he was not enough of a machinist. So the carpenter would have ended by keeping all the laurels, but that he was deprived of them in a most unexpected way. A well known dramatist taking his seat in the stalls the other night remarked to the spruce young female attendant who distributed the programmes, "That earthquake idea was a very fine one of —" he was not able to finish his sentence. "Oh, thank you, sir," she exclaimed with effusion, and retired blushing and triumphant.

A play on King Arthur and his Round Table by Mr. Wills is announced to follow *Macbeth* at the Lyceum, with Ellen Terry as Guinevere. There was a rumor going the rounds some time ago that he had written a *Robert Emmet* for Irving, and that the censor interfered. It is probably a canard.

One day Mr. Burnand, the editor of Punch and general critic and wit, was sitting reading a newspaper in the Savile Club, a place of general resort for men of letters, Messrs. Austin Dobson, Edmund Gosse and Herbert Spencer being among its more constant frequenters. Mr. Wills came in. Now Mr. Burnand had just damned a play of his and so was careful to bury his head in the paper. "I have something to say that very much concerns Mr. Burnand," said the dramatist, leaning his back against the fire. The editor of Punch looked up. Mr. Willis went on: "You will remember Dutton Cook, and how he was always damning my plays and Miss S——'s acting? [Mr. Burnand remembered.] One day I said to Miss S——, 'Let us make a little wax image of Dutton Cook'; we made it. 'Now, let us melt it before the fire and stick pins in it'; we did so. Next day I met a friend, and he said to me, 'Have you heard the news — Dutton Cook is dead?'" Having finished his story, Mr. Wills went out, and since that day Mr. Burnand, who is no less superstitious than witty, is said to have only abused Mr. Wills' plays in reason.

I wonder are all the cheap reprints of good books read as well as bought. A very distinguished poet who has always issued his own poems at very high prices said in my hearing the other day that he believed the cheap books were only bought for their cheapness. A friend of his once purchased, he said, a London Directory twenty years old because he could get it for threepence: it was such a large book for the money. I hope the three-penny reprint of Aubrey de Vere's beautiful

Legends of St. Patrick, just issued by Cassell, Petter & Galpin, will have a kinder fate and be read as well as bought. It will probably sell by tens of thousands, if one can at all judge by the immense sale of the same publishers' threepenny editions of such poems as Coventry Patmore's *Angel in the House*, and the sculptor Woolner's *Beautiful Lady*. Its being reprinted at all is a sign of the times. A few years ago no Englishman would look at any Irish book unless to revile it. *Ça ira.*

Apropos of poets, the peasant poet is less common in England than with us in Ireland, but I did meet the other day an Englishman who was a true specimen of the tribe. He is a Mr. Skipsey. He is from the coal country — a strange nursing mother for a poet — and taught himself to write by scribbling with a piece of white chalk on the sides of coal shafts and galleries. In the depth of a mine hundreds of feet under the earth he has written many of his sweetest and tenderest songs. He has not been left to sing his songs to the dull ear of the mine, however. The most sensitive ears of our time have heard them. Rossetti, a little before his death, read and praised these simple poems. The last few months Walter Scott's collection of Mr. Skipsey's mining poems has made new admirers for their au-

thor. He is more like a sailor than a miner,
but like a sailor who is almost painfully sensitive and refined. He talked to me about Clar-
ence Mangan a good deal. Mangan is a great
favorite of his. He recited, for the benefit of
a Saxon who stood by, Mangan's Dark Rosaleen. Himself a peasant, he turned for the
moment's inspiration to the country where
poetry has been a living voice among the
people.

There has been some talk lately in the Parnell Commission about the Clondalkin Branch
of the National League. Archbishop Walsh
in his evidence mentioned it as the only
branch whose action he had been compelled
to condemn. They had written up a black list
of people they did not approve of. When I
was last in Ireland I saw a good deal of the
main mover in the matter. Not at all a fire-
brand, one would think, but a quiet shoe-
maker, who had read and thought a great
deal. I used often to stray into his shop to
have a chat about books, among the leather
clippings. Since then I have seen at odd
times in Irish papers sketches and stories of
peasant character by him, all full of keen ob-
servation. Carlyle, Emerson and Miss Laffan
are his favorite authors. When I saw him last
he was struggling with Emerson's Over-Soul,

but told me that he always read Carlyle when
"wild with the neighbors." Perhaps his black
list was only a piece of Carlylese. The bi-
ographer of Frederick did so love the strong
hand! Though, indeed, most men of letters
seem to have a tendency towards an amateur-
ish love of mere strength. They grow impa-
tient of the slow progress of thought perhaps,
and long to touch the hilt of the sword.

I have some literary news from Ireland.
Mr. T. W. Rolleston, who has just translated
Walt Whitman into German, is now busy on
a life of Lessing for Mr. Walter Scott, who
published last autumn the shilling reprint of
his translation from Epictetus. Mr. Rolleston
has just removed to Dublin from his pretty
Wicklow house, where for years now he has
been busy with his beehives and Walt Whitman. He is a fine Greek scholar and quite
the handsomest man in Ireland, but I wish
he would devote his imagination to some national purpose. Cosmopolitan literature is,
at best, but a poor bubble, though a big one.
Creative work has always a fatherland.

Miss O'Leary is preparing for the press a
collection of her poems. Her friends, who
have undertaken all business matters concerning the book, have decided to have for frontis-
pieces photographs of Miss O'Leary and Mr.

John O'Leary. There will be an introduction
describing their life and connection with the
old Fenian movement, and, by way of appen-
dix, Sir Charles Gavan Duffy's article on
Miss O'Leary's poems. They are, indeed,
tender and beautiful verses — Irish alike in
manner and matter. One of the most, if not
the most, distinguished of critics now writing
in the English tongue once said to me, though
he did not in the least sympathize with her
national aspirations, "Miss O'Leary's poems,
like Wordsworth's, have the rarest of all gifts
— a true simplicity." Nothing quite like
them has been printed anywhere since Kickham wrote, "She lived beside the Anner."
They are the last notes of that movement of
song, now giving place to something new, that
came into existence when Davis, singing,
rocked the cradle of a new Ireland. We of the
younger generation owe a great deal to Mr.
John O'Leary and his sister. What nationality is in the present literary movement in
Ireland is largely owing to their influence —
an influence all feel who come across them.
The material for many a song and ballad has
come from Mr. John O'Leary's fine collection
of Irish books — the best I know. The whole
house is full of them. One expects to find
them bulging out of the windows. He, more

clearly than any one, has seen that there is no fine nationality without literature, and seen the converse also, that there is no fine literature without nationality.

August 3, 1889

LADY WILDE

LONDON has been empty a long while now, all folk who could having fled to the continent or Brighton or elsewhither in search of green fields and sea winds. They will soon be on their way home, with much secret satisfaction, for your Londoner, in spite of all he may say, does not much care for the country. He is not used to be alone, and considers the joys of country solitude a fiction of the poets, all the pleasanter to read about because it is only fiction and no reality questioning his own noisy and talkative existence.

Lady Wilde still keeps up, in spite of London's emptiness, her Saturday afternoon receptions, though the handful of callers contrasts mournfully with the roomful of clever people one meets there in the season. There is no better time, however, to hear her talk than now, when she is unburdened by weary guests, and London has few better talkers.

When one listens to her and remembers that Sir William Wilde was in his day a famous *raconteur*, one finds it no way wonderful that Oscar Wilde should be the most finished talker of our time. Lady Wilde has known most of our '48 poets and novelists — Carleton, Lover, Lever and the rest, and can say something vital and witty of them all. She has a pile of Carleton's letters and can tell many things of our great humorist whose heart was so full of tears. She never saw Davis, but some one described to me how his funeral gave her a first impulse towards nationalism. She was walking through Grafton Street (I think it was), when a great crowd came by following a hearse. It seemed as though the crowd would never end. She stepped inside a bookshop to let it pass. The crowds still streamed by. "Whose funeral is this?" she asked the shop-boy. "The funeral of Thomas Davis," was the answer. "Who was Thomas Davis?" "A poet," was the reply. It seemed to her there must be something great and imaginative in a country where so many followed a poet to the grave. Thenceforth she began to think deeply on these matters; the result soon came in the poems of "Speranza." This story has never been printed before.

Lady Wilde would do good service if she would write her memoirs, the appearance and ways of our '48 men are often so scantily known to us. Many a writer of incomparable song and ballad has no more record than his voice. We do not know even whether he was witty or wearisome, dark or fair. A hundred years hence men will peer about in vain for any history of Keegan, the farm laborer; and concerning Edward Walsh they will find no more, or little more, than that he used to wander about the roads near Dublin, a little harp on his left arm.

Lady Wilde could fill many blank spaces. Meanwhile, she is doing good work in setting down in good English Sir William Wilde's great collection of folk-lore and legend. Sir William Wilde employed peasants in all parts of Ireland to gather together everything in the way of charm or fairy tale. Old men and women, too, when going away cured from his hospital, would ask leave to send him eggs or fowl, or some such country gift, and he would bargain for a fairy tale instead. Lady Wilde is now preparing for the press a new volume taken from this great collection. It will be of some size, and deal mainly with charms and spells.

Two other writers are about to publish with

David Nutt books on Irish folk and fairy lore
— David Fitzgerald and Douglas Hyde.
Fitzgerald's articles in La Revue Celtique
promise well for his volume, some of the
stories being most curious and weird, though
spoiled a good deal by the absence of any attempt to give the native idiom they were told
in. They are written more from the side of
science than literature. Douglas Hyde's, on
the other hand, will be, I feel sure, the most
Irish of all folk-lore. He understands perfectly the language of the people and writes it
naturally, as others do book-English. Most
of the stories in his forthcoming book have
already appeared in the original Gaelic in his
Leabhar Sgeulaighteachta. The three stories
he translated for *Fairy and Folk Tales of the
Irish Peasantry* show what a master he is of
dialect. He is surely the most imaginative of
all Irish scholars, and I believe these wild and
sombre stories of his will make some noise in
the world.

Douglas Hyde also has on hand a little
Gaelic book on the famous musician and poet,
Carolan. He will give therein a number of
anecdotes and unpublished verses gathered
among the old men of Connaught. I hope he
will take pity on us poor folk who have no
Gaelic and translate it some day. He owes us

also a volume of his own ballads. His contributions to *Poems and Ballads of Young Ireland*, 1888, and the new and very unequal *Lays and Lyrics of the Pan-Celtic Society* (a book that has lain too short a time on my table for any more detailed verdict now) are full of true Gaelic flavor.

The new publishing season, however, will bring forth much more than goblin, witch and fairy legends. Sir Charles Gavan Duffy's long expected life of Thomas Davis alone would make it a red letter season for us. Its author is now working away in a house near Park Lane at the last two chapters, and the whole will be in Kegan Paul's hands in a week or two.

Kegan Paul will publish also a work on the treatment of Irish political prisoners by Dr. Sigerson of Dublin, well known in Ireland and elsewhere as a physician, publicist and historian. A great portion of the book appeared piecemeal in the Dublin Freeman's Journal, but well deserves preservation in the more permanent book form. Dr. Sigerson was a member of the last commission of inquiry into prisons and prison discipline, and is necessarily thoroughly acquainted with his subject. He has, besides, a very large knowledge of Irish history, statistics and the like, and that shaping brain which knows how to use its materials.

So much for forthcoming books. Among those just published are two of some importance on the same subject as Dr. Sigerson's. The first is issued from the office of The Freeman's Journal, and edited by Mr. E. Dwyer Gray, and has a preface by Sir C. G. Duffy, who, however, in no way vouches for the contents of the book, which he has apparently not read, but simply expresses his views on the general question. The book is mostly made up of a reprint of the various letters on the subject addressed to The Freeman by foreign, colonial and other gentlemen of more or less importance in their respective countries. It would, however, be very much the better for a good deal of boiling down, for while some of the letters are of very great importance and some of less, a great many are simply of no importance whatever.

The second book is from the hands of an ex-Cabinet Minister, Mr. Shaw Lefevre, and is chockful of facts and figures somewhat dryasdustically arranged, like all Mr. Shaw Lefevre writes. This may be said to be good work but bad workmanship. It is, however, useful, as all his books are, and valuable as an admission from the English Radical standpoint of iniquitous treatment of political prisoners by England, both in the past and the present.

This letter has been somewhat bookish, but then, as I explained, the season is over and every one has fled from town and left me no gossip of men and things any way up-to-date. Also the book time is near at hand — another season than that of London has come to an end — the season of swifts and swallows. They are now all flying southward, piercing the dew by the Pillars of Hercules or gathering together on house tops preparing for their journey. The trees are turning gold and red and yellow, and the whole appearance of the outer world makes one grow mindful of the fireside. And thither this coming winter all reading Irishmen will certainly take *The Life of Thomas Davis*, and when the witching hour has come and ghosts are creeping about, if they be wise, they will open Hyde's translated *Leabhar Sgeulaighteachta*. These two volumes, one of the old generation, the other of the new, will, I imagine, be the events of the season for us.

September 28, 1889

THE THREE O'BYRNES

WE HAVE all been saddened by Miss O'Leary's sudden death on the fifteenth of this month. The death of this heroic woman who lived ever, in the words of her own song, written of another, "to God and Ireland true," has left a sore place in numerous hearts. Everywhere sympathy is felt for her brother, Mr. John O'Leary, whose lifelong friend and ally she was.

This is Hallow Eve night, the night of fairies, and opportune to the occasion a paper comes to hand with a report of Colonel Olcott's lectures, last week in Dublin, on our Irish goblins. He asserted that such things really exist, and so strangely has our modern world swung back on its old belief, so far has the reaction from modern materialism gone, that his audience seemed rather to agree with him. He returns to London at once, where the faithful of his creed are busy with many strange schemes — among the rest the establishing of an occult monastery in Switzerland, where all devout students of the arcane sciences may bury themselves from the world for a time or forever.

H. P. Blavatsky, the pythoness of the Movement, holds nightly levees at Lansdowne Road. She is certainly a woman of great learning and character. A London wit once described her as the low comedian of the world to come. This unkind phrase, anything but an accurate account of this strange woman, had this much truth, that she can always enjoy a joke even against herself. The other day she was returning from Jersey, whither she had gone for her health. A young man from Birmingham began talking to her. "They are a rum lot, them theosophists," he said. "Yes, a rum lot," she replied. "And that rum old woman at the head of them," he went on. "That rum old woman, H. P. Blavatsky, has now the honor of speaking to you." "Ah! I do not mean that old woman," he stammered out, "but another old woman."

Apropos of the fairies, a friend brings me a strange story from Donegal. It has nearly made him a believer in the actual existence of the creatures, like Colonel Olcott, whom Andrew Lang called the other day "the Fairies' Friend." He was poking about in a rath at the foot of Slieve League, in Donegal, and seeing a large hole, asked what made it. "That is where the three O'Byrnes dig for treasure," a countryman told him. Presently a shoeless man, with ragged hair and ragged clothes, came up and began working at the hole with a crowbar. He asked who it was. "The third O'Byrne," was the answer. He spoke to the man, who only shook his head — he knew only Gaelic. The people about told my friend, who was staying in their village, the story of the treasure. It was buried long ago under a ban. Three O'Byrnes had in succession to seek it and die just at the moment of its discovery, but when the last had died it would be the possession of their heirs forever. Two had already died, the first torn to pieces by a phantom dog that came rushing down the mountain; the second saw the treasure and was driven mad by some terrible apparition and died. Now the third sought all day long, time after time; my friend saw him at work. He would die, he knew, but the O'Byrnes would be enriched.

A German translation of Miss Katharine Tynan's poems has just appeared. The translator's name is Fräulein Clara Commer of Breslau, and the volume is dedicated by special permission to the Empress's mother, Augusta. The translation is, I hear, a very good one. Miss Tynan herself has just returned to Ireland after a long stay in London, and the stream of callers will have commenced again, on Sunday afternoons, to pour into the pretty thatched Clondalkin farmhouse.

I announced in my last letter the forthcoming life of Davis. It will be preceded a week or two by the Camelot edition of his essays, which will be published on December first. The editor is Mr. T. W. Rolleston, who has had all through the assistance of Sir Charles Gavan Duffy.

A short while since, literary London was deeply moved by the suicide of the young Jewish novelist and verse writer, Miss Amy Levy. Many will take up with sad interest the posthumous volume, *A London Plane-Tree*, now in the press. She and her works are so typical of our day. Social problems have made us melancholy, and the old resting places for the mind have been swept away. Any poor heart otherwise overladen has a hard time of it. Miss Levy had much in her own life to make her unhappy, and all the fretfulness of our age bore in upon her as well. One day she could stand it no longer, and so shut to her door and her window, and lighted a pan of charcoal and died. Fame that so long had turned from her awoke round her grave. *Reuben Sachs*, her sad Jewish novel, has found its meed of notability now. Man will turn anywhere where life is, anywhere rather than the dull round of meals and newspapers, even towards a heart so strewn with salt and bit-

terness that Lethe and its darkness seemed
sweeter far than youth and all its possibil-
ities. Miss Levy's poems many times dwell
on the thought of suicide, dwell on it in a simple matter-of-fact way, without sentimental-
ity. Here is a little poem, published six years
ago, and called A Cross Road Epitaph:

> When first the world grew dark to me,
> I call'd on God, yet came not He.
> Whereon, as wearier waxed my lot,
> On Love I call'd, but Love came not;
> When a worse evil did befall,
> Death, on thee only I did call.

The burthen of her poetry is ever much the
same, and yet she never seems to assume
wretchedness for effect. One verse struck me
as having an unusual force:

> Of warmth and sun and sweetness,
>   All nature takes a part;
> The ice of all the ages
>   Weighs down upon my heart.

The immediate cause, if any, of her suicide we
may never know. The veil will cover it. I
saw her no long while before her death. She
was talkative, good-looking in a way and full
of the restlessness of the unhappy. Had she
cared to live, a future of some note awaited
her. Her poetry (her prose I have but glanced
at) showed a strong literary faculty, not so

much poetic as tending to the precise, definite thoughts that make good prose, and sometimes rising by sheer intensity to the region of poetry.

Two other books full of present day world sadness have just reached me, and both by Irish ladies. The first is Miss Ryan's poems, *Songs of Remembrance*, the second an advance copy of Miss Keeling's prose sketches *In Thoughtland and Dreamland*. Miss Keeling seems to have picked up her world sadness, like the swallow in Mrs. Carlyle's poem, under German eaves, and Miss Ryan hers maybe on the benches of her own village chapel; yet both are alike in being a little sentimental. Indeed Miss Keeling is not a little sentimental, but very much so. There is scarcely anything in the world she would not drop a tear on. Miss Ryan can write very prettily sometimes, as thus:

> On earth and sky and far-off sea,
>   It is a lovely tender hour:
>   A sweet virgin crowned with gracious power.
> To-night in heaven what must it be!

The notion of heaven sharing somehow the more gentle changes of earth receives a new thought and a pleasant one. Miss Ryan is one of the little group of poets who surround The Irish Monthly, one of the same school

with Miss Tynan, Miss Mulholland, the late
Attie O'Brien and others who have made religion their most common inspiration. She is
too sad by a great deal. Most good poets have
much sadness in them, but then they keep it
more implicit than explicit. It comes in spite
of them; they do not fondle it and pet it.

In this matter Miss Keeling's sins are even
greater. She seems to have read second-rate
German romances without end. Her whole
book is simply a huge, iridescent tear; but it
is really iridescent. The style always glitters.
It glitters too much, indeed. It has more of
the gleam of drawing-room candelabra than
the soft lustre of nature. She has genuine wit,
though, and power of description. Old ladies
at lodging-houses, old maids, children, door-
step cleaners, maids-of-all-work, lady artists in
reduced circumstances, sentimental Germans,
the whole squalid rabble of the lodging house,
pass by, drawn with much real vigor. Miss
Keeling has been everywhere and seen everything and may yet write good novels—though,
indeed, I am told she has already done this in
Two Sisters. She is young and ardently Irish
— witness the very pretty chapters on Ireland
in the present volume. One must be on the
watch to see what may come out of this glit-
tering faculty of hers. She must, though, give

up the iridescent tear. It is not her own, it is stolen goods. Meanwhile she should go over to Ireland and see what she can find there to write about. After all, Ireland is the true subject for the Irish.

November 23, 1889

CHEVALIER BURKE AND SHULE AROON

I HAVE just been reading Mr. R. L. Stevenson's *Master of Ballantrae*. We Irish people have a bone to pick with him for his sketch of the blackguard adventurer, Chevalier Burke. I do not feel sure that the Chevalier is not a true type enough, but Mr. Stevenson is certainly wrong in displaying him for a typical Irishman. He is really a broken-down Norman gentleman, a type found only among the gentry who make up what is called "the English garrison." He is from the same source as the Hell Fire Club and all the reckless braggadocio of the eighteenth century in Ireland; one of that class who, feeling the uncertainty of their tenures, as Froude explains it, lived the most devil-may-care existence. One sometimes meets even at this day vulgar, plausible, swaggering "Irishmen," who are its much decayed survivals, and who give Mr. Stevenson his justification. They are bad, but none of our making; English settlers bore them, English laws moulded them. No one who knows the serious, reserved and suspicious Irish peasant ever held them in any way representative of the national type. It is clear that Mr. Stevenson has no first hand knowledge of Ireland, and when a member of the English garrison, private or subaltern, comes to England and chooses to masquerade as a genuine Irishman, he too often, through some perversion of moral judgment, affects to be some such Irishman as this rogue and charlatan and mountebank "gentleman," Chevalier Burke. I do not, of course, assert more than that there is a bad tradition amongst the English garrison of which the mean and reckless nature takes advantage.

Mr. Stevenson puts into the mouth of the Chevalier a curious version of Shule Aroon, which he seems to suppose the correct one. Before the publication of *The Master* I heard from a common friend that he would use this version, and wrote at once to a well known authority on Irish songs about it and got the answer I expected, that it was a Scotch or North of Ireland variation, and certainly much later than the words given by Gavan

Duffy. It is a corruption, but a pretty one. I have the whole somewhere, but have mislaid it. Here is the verse quoted in *The Master*:

> O, I will dye my petticoat red,
> With my dear boy I'll beg my bread,
> Though all my friends should wish me dead,
> For Willie among the rushes, O!

The same verse in the old version goes thus:

> I'll dye my petticoats, I'll dye them red,
> And round the world I'll beg my bread,
> Until my parents shall wish me dead,
> Is go d-teidh tu, a mhuirnin, slan! [1]

"For Willie among the rushes, O!" is beautiful. I wish we could claim it.

Apropos of novels, a publisher told me the other day that he constantly had orders for complete editions of the *Tales by the O'Hara Family*, but finds that the best novels of the brothers Banim are out of print, while some of the worst are still selling merrily. The same is true of Carleton, as far at least as Ireland is concerned. I have made some inquiries and find that some of the worst books he wrote, books written to raise the wind in his time of decadence, are still in print and selling steadily, while his greatest novels, *Fardorougha* and *The Black Prophet*, the two greatest of all

[1] "And mayest thou go, my little darling, safe!"

Irish stories, can only be found on the second-hand bookstalls. The ways of publishers are mysterious. You are more lucky in America. I saw both novels in a book list in The Pilot the other day. But why do you miscall *Fardorougha*, "Farah"?

There was a great autograph sale at Sotheby's last week. Letters of Sheridan's, Burke's, Goldsmith's, Beaconsfield's, Shelley's, Lamb's and Blake's were put to the hammer. One heard the market value of many a great name. The old man at the high desk has seen the rise and fall of many reputations. His little wooden hammer has registered the degrees of many a decadence. When he was young, Bulwer Lytton must have been at his zenith, his name in all men's mouths, but

> The secret worm ne'er ceases,
> Nor the mouse behind the wall.

The other day his black hammer knocked down an unpublished history of the Lytton family, thirty-one pages long, written by the late Lord Lytton himself, for no more than three pounds, ten shillings, not half what a single letter of Blake's fetched; yet Blake, when he was alive, had no fame at all, and lived constantly close down to the zero, starvation. He and his wife had for some time no more than ten shillings a week between them.

For a copy of his poem, *America*, illustrated with what we know to be the most beautiful of his designs, and all colored by hand, he could then get no more than half — it would fetch fifty times the price now — the eight pounds, ten shillings paid for this letter written in shaking strokes by his dying hand. Other letters of his fetched good prices, but this was the most beautiful of all the letters, his own and other people's.

"I have been very near the gates of death," it goes, "and have returned very weak, and an old man feeble and tottering, but not in spirits and life, not in the real man, the imagination which liveth forever. In that I am stronger and stronger as this foolish body decays. . . . Flaxman is gone, and we must all soon follow, everyone to his own eternal house." A letter of George Meredith's was put up and sold for five pounds. A dealer who had bid five shillings seemed greatly surprised. Meredith was a new star. "Who is he?" he muttered. "He must be bidding himself." Among the letters were several from kings and princes. On the whole, potentates went dirt cheap. As I came into the room the auctioneer was crying out, "Any advance on eight shillings for Joseph Bonaparte?"

We have lost an Irish writer whose emi-

nence will be more visible a hundred years
hence than it is to-day. The papers have just
chronicled the death of the poet Allingham.
Shortly before his death he published the last
volume of a complete edition of his poems in,
I think, four volumes: one volume of short
Irish poems and two of miscellaneous lyrics,
and one containing *Laurence Bloomfield*, the
long agrarian poem Gladstone so much liked.
They were brought out by Reeves & Turner.
It is not by his long poems he will live. He
was the Herrick of the century. Time will
take but little toll from his best lyrics; they
are a possession for Ireland for ever. His
native Ballyshannon will some day be very
fond indeed of this child of hers, and may even
be a place of literary pilgrimage some day. He
will make the little town he loved very familiar to the twentieth century, the little town he
sang of so wistfully:

> A wild west Coast, a little Town,
> Where little Folk go up and down,
> Tides flow and winds blow:
> Night and Tempest and the Sea,
> Human Will and Human Fate:
> What is little, what is great?
> Howsoe'er the answer be,
> Let me sing of what I know.

Time has taken a great deal from us this
autumn. William Allingham was to most of

us merely a distant celebrity, a literary influence. So far as his being alive affected us personally it was merely with irritation at the constant changes for the worse he made in his poems; but Miss O'Leary's austere and sweet face was very near to the heart of most of us Irish scribbling folk. It will be a good while before Dublin seems the same again to the writer of this note. All that was most noble and upright in Irish things was dear to her. The good of Ireland was her constant thought. As a friend she ever drew from one the best one had. She, like her brother, was of the old heroic generation now passing away, the generation whose efforts for Ireland made the present movement possible. Our movement may surpass theirs in success; it will never equal it in self-sacrifice. She had the manner of one who had seen something of great affairs and shared in them, yet under all was a heart ever delighted with simple things, a heart from which rose a little wellspring of song. Her poetry had in its mingled austerity and tenderness a very Celtic quality. It was like a rivulet flowing from mountain snows. She was her brother's lifelong friend and fellow-worker. One thinks of him now sitting among his books in the house at Drumcondra.

December 28, 1889

BROWNING

THE one literary topic of these latter weeks is, of course, Browning. A great deal — wise and foolish — has been written about him in all the papers, and a great many anecdotes hunted out of the obscure places of people's memories and well dusted and set upon their legs again. Our newspapers and popular preachers seem all to have fastened on Browning's optimism as the one thing about him specially to be commended, and to have magnified it into a central mood. I was talking recently with a great friend of Browning's, who insisted that this way of taking him as a kind of sermon-maker was quite false, that he was only an optimist because he was an artist who chose hopefulness as his method of expression, and that he could be pessimistic when the mood seized him. I think, though going rather too far, there is a good deal of truth in this: thought and speculation were to Browning means of dramatic expression much more than aims in themselves. He did speak out his own thoughts sometimes though — dramatized Robert Browning. I like to think of the great reverie of the Pope in *The Ring and the Book*, with all its serenity and quietism, as something that came straight from Browning's own mind, and gave his own final judgment on many things. But nearly always he evades giving a direct statement by what he called his dramatic method. It is hard to know when he is speaking or when it is only one of his *dramatis personae*. An acquaintance of mine said once to him, "Mr. Browning, you are a mystic." "Yes," he answered, "but how did you find it out?"

To Browning thought was mainly interesting as an expression of life. In life in all its phases he seems to have had the most absorbing interest; no man of our day has perhaps approached him there. In a thinker like Herbert Spencer one finds, I imagine, Browning's opposite. Spencer probably cares little for life, except as an expression of thought. He lives in boarding houses surrounded by endless clatter and chatter, but has proved himself equal to the occasion. He has had two buttons, or things like buttons, designed by an artist and made exactly to fit his ears. When the clatter and chatter grows too great, he simply thrusts in the buttons and is at once deaf as a post. Eager lion hunters may gather round in vain; he smiles and says, "Yes, yes," but all the time his mind is far off, thinking those abstract generalizations of his. To Robert Browning the world was simply a great boarding house in which people come and go in a confused kind of way. The clatter and chatter to him was life, was joy itself. Sometimes the noise and restlessness got too much into his poetry, and the expression became confused and the verse splintered and broken.

Somewhere in *Wilhelm Meister's Apprenticement* it is told how a father went to see his son, who was being taught at a kind of ideal Goethean school. The master pointed out to him a cloud on the horizon; when it came nearer he saw that it was dust raised by his son who was training horses. The master explained that the boy had proved most fitted to be a groom, and so a groom he was made. A school has just been started in the Peak District of Derbyshire where such a thing might really happen. The prospectus, artistically bound in brown paper and stamped with the five-pointed star of the occultists, is now lying before me. The pupils are to be brought up according to socialistic ideas, taught manual work as well as book learning, and be made accustomed to do everything for themselves. Each boy will be educated, not according to any hard and fast rule or system forced on all as in other schools, but according to the tendencies he shows, whether they be to follow the plow or paint pictures, to train horses or write histories.

Edward Carpenter, the founder, is one of the most picturesque thinkers of the day. He was a fellow of Oxford, with good prospects of all kinds, but found himself getting sadder and sadder. Stepniak met him and turned to a bystander, and said, "That young man is like one of our young Russian anarchists who have a great deal on their minds." Carpenter has turned out a teacher of what must seem to many strangely anarchic notions. Some time after Stepniak saw him he got ill. Some one gave him a copy of Walt Whitman's *Leaves of Grass*. It changed his whole life. When he got well he gave up his fellowship and bought a little patch of land in Derbyshire, where he grew vegetables and sold them on his own hand cart with his own hands for a living. He built a small cottage for himself, and there he and his wife lived. They have found, he believes, the true basis of happiness in simplicity of life, and a proper mingling of manual and mental labor. From time to time this English Thoreau preaches his opinions in essays printed in various more or less socialistic magazines. The last one, Civilization: Its Cause and Cure, has made some small stir.

Messrs. Little, Brown & Company of Boston have kindly sent me some advance sheets of a book to be called *Irish Myths and Folklore*. The author is Mr. Jeremiah Curtin. When the completed book comes I will review it at length, for it promises to be the most careful and scientific work on Irish folk-lore yet published. The introduction is most interesting, and contrasts strikingly with the introduction to Campbell's *Tales of the Western Highlands*, the great Scotch folk-lore book. Campbell was an imaginative man and a good writer, but his long introduction leaves me at any rate rather bored. Mr. Curtin is not less scientific, but the whole science of folk-lore has grown more imaginative these last twenty years. To the old folk-lorists, fables and fairy tales were a haystack of dead follies, wherein the virtuous might find one little needle of historical truth. Since then Joubainville and Rhys and many more have made us see in all these things old beautiful mythologies wherein ancient man said symbolically all he knew about God and man's soul, once famous religions fallen into ruin and turned into old wives' tales, but still luminous from the rosy dawn of human reverie.

Another folk-lore book I have just been dipping into is Lady Wilde's just published *Ancient Cures, Charms, and Usages of Ireland*.

I have had no time to do more at present than read the chapter on Irish proverbs at the end. They are full of a kind of half-Oriental tenderness and fancifulness. A proverb like the following might have come from Saadi: "The lake is not encumbered by its swan; nor the steed by its bridle; nor the sheep by its wool; nor the man by the soul that is in him." This, too, is quite as fine: "God is nigher to us even than the door. God stays long, but He strikes at last." It seems less Oriental because it makes us think of an Irish peasant's cabin where the door is very near. I will return to this book. I want to remind Irish-American readers of the books of folk-lore that are just out or coming. The newly awakened interest in all things Irish is serving our folk-lore well. We have now these *Ancient Cures*, published this week; a little later will come Mr. Curtin's book; then Mr. Nutt of London will bring out Mr. David Fitzgerald's long expected volume, and Dr. Douglas Hyde's English and enlarged edition of his Gaelic *Leabhar Sgeulaighteachta*. Dr. Hyde, if he comes up to my expectations, will give us the most completely Irish folk-lore book, both in manner and matter, that has yet come from any press. He has already given us in Teig O'Kane the best told folk-tale in our literature.

A friend of mine was at Trinity College, Dublin, with a brother of the late William Allingham's, and tells me that Allingham's literary sensitiveness was then greatly troubled by a custom his brother had of writing poems and publishing them in the Ballyshannon papers by way of joke with the name William Allingham at the foot. When one remembers his fastidiousness and his constant habit of polishing and re-polishing all he wrote, one can well imagine his indignation. Another brother is now a doctor in Belfast and wrote a capital letter to The Freeman the other day, saying that William Allingham's best work was Irish and that he would have written far more effectively in every sense had he remained in Ireland in touch with the people; and that had he done so his political sympathies would certainly have widened instead of remaining ever at the *Laurence Bloomfield* stage. This letter is the truest thing yet written about this most delicate of our poets. Allingham had the making of a great writer in him, but lacked impulse and momentum, the very things national feeling could have supplied. Whenever an Irish writer has strayed away from Irish themes and Irish feeling, in almost all cases he has done no more than make alms for oblivion. There is no great literature without nationality, no great nationality without literature.

February 22, 1890

IRELAND'S HEROIC AGE

DR. TODHUNTER of Trinity College, Dublin, has written a charming little pastoral drama, called *A Sicilian Idyll*, and founded on a story in Theocritus. He is bringing it out early in May at the little club theatre here, in this red-bricked and red-tiled suburb, Bedford Park, where so many of us writing people have gathered. It is certainly one of the best things he has written, and has had the good fortune to fall into the hands of a decidedly strong company of mingled amateurs and professionals. I have never heard verse better spoken than by the lady who takes the part of the shepherdess heroine, Amaryllis, and the singing of the chorus of shepherds and shepherdesses — so far as my untechnical ear can judge — rings out finely. The music is being written and superintended through the rehearsal by Mr. Luard-Selby, the author of a number of well known songs and the beautiful church service used in Salisbury Cathedral. The whole play, with its graceful and many-colored Greek costumes, will make a charming

unity with the quaint little theatre, with its
black panels covered with gilt cupids. If successful, and there is every likelihood of its
rousing even more interest than Professor
Herkomer's yearly play at Bushey, there is
some talk of getting up an annual venture of
this same kind, a sort of May Day festival
of dramatic poetry. What the play next year
will be I cannot say; at present all concerned
are deep in Arcadia. In every corner of Dr.
Todhunter's study are shepherd crooks and
long sticks topped with pine cones to serve as
wands for the shepherd priests of Bacchus,
who in the first scene enter in slow procession
carrying the image of the god and singing his
praises, and on the chairs are colored silks to
be made into stately costumes.

The play seems to me much more interesting than his previous drama, *Helena in Troas*,
and *Helena* was very successful, its eloquent
verse and incomparable staging having made
it the feature of its season. The present poem,
one need hardly say, is being got up in nothing
like so elaborate a manner. Its fine verse will,
I believe, quite make amends, and Dr. Todhunter will have as many requests for leave to
revive it as in the case of the larger work, and
will feel readier to consent. He has several
times refused leave to ambitious amateurs

who wished to perform *Helena*, in the belief that their resources would be only equal to making it absurd. In one case he consented. It was acted at Exeter in connection with the University Extension Lectures. There is now more talk of its revival in America at a regular theatre and on a proper scale.

Anything that brings, even for a moment, good verse onto the stage is certainly a desirable thing, and yet these Greek plays do not seem to me quite the most valuable work Dr. Todhunter might do just now. They have at best but a reflected glory — modern imitation of the antique. Mr. Justin McCarthy, in an article last week, said that Irishmen leave little impression on contemporary literature — they are absorbed into journalism and politics. This is true, unhappily, though he did not mention all the things that absorb us. Cosmopolitanism is one of the worst. We are not content to dig our own potato patch in peace. We peer over the wall at our neighbor's instead of making our own garden green and beautiful. And yet it is a good garden and there have been great transactions within it, from the death of Cuchulain down to the flight of Michael Dwyer from the burning cabin. Dr. Todhunter could easily have found some pastoral incident among its stories

newer and not less beautiful than anything
in Tempe's fabled vales.

The first thing needful if an Irish literature
more elaborate and intense than our fine but
primitive ballads and novels is to come into
being is that readers and writers alike should
really know the imaginative periods of Irish
history. It is not needful that they should
understand them with scholars' accuracy, but
they should know them with the heart, so as
not to be repelled by what is strange and
outré in poems or plays or stories taken therefrom. The most imaginative of all our periods
was the heroic age and the few centuries that
followed it and preceded the Norman Invasion — a time of vast and mysterious shadows, like the clouds heaped round a sun rising
from the sea. Anyone who knew Standish
O'Grady's *History of Ireland: The Heroic Period*, and Lady Ferguson's *Ireland Before the
Conquest*, and perhaps Mrs. Bryant's *Celtic
Ireland* (taking care to forget her prosaic and
baseless notions about the early races) would
have a very fair knowledge of the time. I am
glad to see that George Bell & Sons have just
issued a new edition of Lady Ferguson's book.
It should be on the shelves of every Irish student. It is quite indispensable for reference,
going as it does, king by king, saint by saint,

and battle by battle, through the ten or twelve centuries from early pagan times to the Strongbow invasion. It is a complete contrast to Mrs. Bryant's volume, published last year. Mrs. Bryant picks out various matters that interest her, the Brehon laws, the coming of Patrick, the bards, and so forth, and writes a chapter upon each. Anyone who really knew these books would soon begin to look about for a chance of reading the great old poems and stories themselves. He would find it a hard thing to do. No publisher has yet ventured to gather into one volume a few of the best translations of the most famous old stories—The Children of Lir, Deirdre and the rest. Even then the best of all would remain hidden — *The Tain Bo* lies translated and unpublished on the shelves of the Royal Irish Academy. There is some demon especially told off to keep from the Irish reading public the most poetic part of their literature. Even Sir Samuel Ferguson's great poem, Conary, not to be confused with *Congal* — a fine but heavy work—cannot be got for less than seven shillings and sixpence, though his poetically unimportant Patrician Papers is buyable for a shilling. Yet, to my mind, Conary is the best poem in modern Irish literature, and Aubrey De Vere has said just the same.

Mr. O'Grady, in his Dublin letter to The Daily Graphic, has been criticizing the Irish wolf hounds at the Royal Dublin Societies' show, from the standpoint of a specialist in the bardic literature. The breeders, he says, are wholly on a false track. The ancient wolf hound was, he believes, certainly parti-colored and probably smooth coated. He quotes the following description of the favorite hound of Finn:

> Yellow feet had Bran, and red ears;
> She had a white spot on her breast;
> The rest of her body was black with this exception,
> She was sprinkled with white over the loins.

By the by, the general tone of these Daily Graphic letters makes it pretty plain that Mr. O'Grady is seeing the error of his ways and growing into a good Nationalist after all. He was always out of place — with his enthusiasm for Irish history — among the West British minority with their would-be cosmopolitanism and actual provincialism. O'Grady's political vagaries have all sprung, it seems to me, from that love of force common among a certain type of literary men. The impatience of minds trained to see further than they can go, to discover far-off ideals before the road that leads to them, are responsible for much of it, and Carlyle for the rest perhaps. It is the fruit of a good quality, but none the less irritating at times, as when, for instance, Mr. Standish O'Grady in his incomparable monograph, *Red Hugh*, writes many pages to glorify extremely murderous Sir John Perrot.

A bundle of about fifty letters written by the peasant poet, John Keegan, author of *Caoch O'Leary*, has just been placed in my hands. None have ever been published. They are full of gloomy interest, biographical and other, and as time goes on I dare say The Pilot will hear more from me on this matter. At present I have but skimmed through their time dimmed pages. He seems to have had scarcely less wretched a life than Mangan. The letters are full of lamentations, now for himself, now for Ireland. He will not hear of hope. "Believe me," he writes (this was in 1847), "the old leaven of Orangeism and anti-Irishism will start up from their graves. . . . England is England still; the Saxon is unchanged — as indomitable as the hyena. Britain is strong, Ireland is prostrate, fallen, nearly annihilated." "If the country does not rise," he writes, "we will be trampled into the unblessed graves of those who have already sunk victims of hunger and disease," and if on the other hand they shake off this "vile torpor of slavery and contented beg-

gary" and take to arms, still he has small
hope, but then at any rate they will be "going
like their fathers of old . . . to die nobly rather
than live as paupers, whining and cringing
slaves"; and he adds, "should such things
happen may I share this glorious privilege."
This letter, one is not surprised to find by the
postscript, was sent to his correspondent by
some little peasant girl whom he could trust,
and not by the post office, a somewhat dan-
gerous place for such unwatered treason.

I am always especially pleased to come
across anything that throws light on the personal side of Irish history or literature in the
way these Keegan letters do. We have paid
far too little attention to it. How many of the
men whose poems delight us in the ballad
books are merely names!

The Fenian period at any rate is now to find
authentic record. We shall learn what manner
of men Stephens and Luby and Kickham and
the others were in the ordinary and extraor-
dinary affairs of life—and learn it, too, from
one of the most polished writers of our time.
Mr. O'Leary is writing his reminiscences, and
his friends are collecting subscribers' names.
I have just been looking through the printed
list and find very different shades of politics.
Interlined with names like Sir Charles Gavan

Duffy, Michael Davitt, William O'Brien, Sir Charles Russell and Professor Galbraith are high Tories like Professor Armstrong, author of the *Stories of Wicklow*, Dean Gwynn and so forth. I see by the evening papers that Mr. Parnell has just added his name. It will be a remarkable list when completed. Seldom have such diverse opinions been represented on the subscription list of a political memoir. Mr. O'Leary's powerful personality has impressed everyone he has come across, and it is now likely that future generations may receive from his written word something of the stimulus his personal presence has been to us.

May 17, 1890

A SICILIAN IDYLL

WILLIAM BLAKE, in one of his little read, or altogether unread, Prophetic Books, has this description of the playgoer at a "tragic scene": "The soul drinks murder and revenge, and applauds its own holiness" — a description that applies, and was surely only meant to apply, to melodrama and its easy victory over our susceptibilities. When we look on at the common drama of murder and sentiment, there is

something about it that flatters us. We iden-
tify ourselves with the hero, and triumph with
him in his soon gained conquest over evil. We
hate the villain, and remember that we are
not as he is. A fine poetic drama, on the other
hand, affects us quite differently. It lifts us
into a world of knowledge and beauty and
serenity. As the Mohammedan leaves his
shoes outside the mosque, so we leave our
selfhood behind before we enter the imper-
sonal temple of art. We come from it with
renewed insight, and with our ideals and our
belief in happiness and goodness stronger
than before. Melodrama can make us weep
more; farce can make us laugh more; but when
the curtain has fallen, they leave nothing behind. They bring us nothing, because they
demand nothing from us. They are excite-
ments, not influences. The poetic drama, on
the other hand, demands so much love of
beauty and austere emotion that it finds un-
certain footing on the stage at best.

Dr. Todhunter is one of the few moderns
who has succeeded in bringing it there even
for a moment. His *Helena in Troas*, a few
years since, was the talk of a London season.
Its sonorous verse, united to the rhythmical
motions of the white-robed chorus, and the
solemnity of burning incense, produced a

semi-religious effect new to the modern stage. He has now come again before that circle of cultivated people who remain faithful to the rightful Muses, and have not bowed the knee to those two slatterns, farce and melodrama, with a little verse play of shepherds and shepherdesses, founded on a story in Theocritus, and called *A Sicilian Idyll*. It has been acted three times — Monday, Wednesday and Friday last — at the little club theatre in Bedford Park, and will be again next Saturday, preliminary to its probable revival elsewhere. The long room with its black panels and gilt Cupids has been crowded with really distinguished audiences.

On Friday I noticed Miss Alma Murray, the creator of the part of Beatrice in the Shelley Society's performance of *Cenci*; Miss Winifred Emery, now performing in Buchanan's *Tom-Boy*; Mr. Cyril Maude; Mr. Terriss, just returned for a time to the Lyceum fold; and Lady Archibald Campbell, of pastoral drama celebrity; and among social and literary notables, Mrs. Jopling Rowe; Miss Mathilde Blind, whose translation of Marie Bashkirtseff's Diary is making a stir just now; Mrs. Charles Hancock, of the Woman's Liberal Association; Mr. Theodore Watts, the critic; and Miss May Morris, daughter of the poet of *The Earthly Paradise*, and herself well known for her embroideries.

The story proved to be a very simple one — the play had just enough action to sustain the verse without letting it seem monotonous, and no more. A proud shepherdess, Amaryllis, is kissed by a shepherd, Alexander, against her will, and before her anger is cool, sees him as she supposes making love to her friend, Thertylis. Believing that he kissed her in mockery, she tries to kill him with an incantation before "it becomes a shepherd's tale." He is brought in dying to her feet. She is at once stricken with remorse. There is only one thing that can save him now, he cries — her love. But did he not woo her friend, Thertylis? "It was but in pretty sport," he answers. Thertylis bid him do so "to move her amorous Daphnis, who stood by." The lovers are reconciled and all goes well. There is also a secondary story that crosses and recrosses the main theme, the story of the love of Thertylis and Daphnis. This meagre plot was made fascinating and absorbing by fine verse, beautiful scenery and picturesque costumes, the shepherds in their leopard skins, and the shepherdesses in their many colored robes, and the scene with its far glimpse of the blue Mediterranean, and its festoons of grape and vine leaves, being a sight to dream of. The play itself was full of human interest and fine poetic passages. It made the Golden Age seem very near. The main impression was one of a divine innocence and youthfulness, the freshness of a world still shining with the dew of dawn. There was one place where the chorus of shepherd youths and maidens, who sing hymns to Bacchus, seemed to strike the keynote of the whole play. They bid Bacchus come crowned "with purple clusters," and they will greet him "with seasonable mirth":

> But come not, as to those who love thee not,
> Thy panther Moenads with their panther kin
> Furiously leaping to the frantic din
> Of clashing cymbals, their flush'd faces hot,
> Smear'd from limbs torn in the glare
> Of blazing torches reeling through the smoke!
> Come, worshipt of our folk,
> Lord of the mellowing year! Come, for we come
> With ankles splash'd with vintage, honouring thee
> With must from foaming vats; bless now thy home,
> Dear as gray Thebes, or Nysa of sweet air,
> Thy own laughing Sicily!

They are a gentle people, living far from clamor and contest, and as we watch them moving to and fro, and dancing their shepherd dances, something of their own innocence seems to sink into the heart. It is this influence, this mood, that lifts the play out of the dust of common life and makes it poetry. It was this that made the audience feel that they had seen something new and memorable, and made the play successful. When the curtain fell, one heard on all sides, "How pretty!" "How beautiful!" "I would not have missed it for the world." It was not merely the play itself that gave one this feeling, for acting, scenery and verse were all a perfect unity. It was like a dream. There were details here and there that I would have wished different, though nothing important enough to take from the charm of the final impression. My literary personality is not the same as Dr. Todhunter's — no two men's are — and I could find fault, here and there, according to my different lights; but where I see so much to admire and be grateful for, I do not care to do otherwise than praise, and will not trouble The Pilot with the few small and mainly verbal changes I should like to see.

The acting deserves a paragraph to itself. Mrs. Edward Emery, who took the part of Amaryllis, won universal praise with her striking beauty and subtle gesture and fine delivery of the verse. Indeed her acting was the feature of the whole performance that struck one most, after the verse itself. I do not know that I have any word too strong

to express my admiration for its grace and
power. Miss Lily Linfield acted the part of
Thertylis with great verve and go, though her
ear for verse was not by any means perfect.
Her dance with cymbals before the statue of
Bacchus was very fine, and well deserved its
enthusiastic encore. The male parts were
taken by amateurs. Mr. Paget, the artist,
looked the athletic Alcander perfectly, and
acted well, though not quite so well as the
versatile and well known gentleman, jour-
nalist, solicitor, lecturer, novelist, authority
on violins, writer on chiromancy and, I believe, war correspondent who prefers to remain hidden under the name of Mr. Smith.
Mr. Paget's part was, however, much the
more difficult. The music for the chorus was
composed by Mr. Luard-Selby, the author of
an admired church service and of a number
of songs. The scenery was painted by Mr.
Baldry and Mr. Arthur Lemon.

June 14, 1890

ROSE KAVANAGH

MISS ROSE KAVANAGH was, when she died,
still a possibility, still — the future. She has
left but a very little bundle of songs and sto-

ries, the mere May blossoming of a young inspiration whose great promise was robbed of fulfillment, first by ill health and then by an early death. Readers of future anthologies of Irish verse will know the name of Kavanagh from Lough Bray and St. Michan's Churchyard, but they will not know the noble, merry and gentle personality that produced them. Death has robbed it of its clear expression. Is there anything sadder than unfulfilled promise? Is it not the very essence of all sadness? It makes one dream that maybe in the world we go to we shall carry to conclusion the tasks left uncompleted in the world we hasten from, that Christian will again take to his scrip and staff in that distant land, but gaily and with perhaps no little exultation.

Miss Rose Kavanagh was born in Tyrone, at Killadroy, in the year 1860. Presently the family moved to Mullaghmore, and the Avonban, the White River, gave place to the many fabled Blackwater, whose wandering course she has celebrated in lines that are tolerably well known through being included in Mr. Sparling's *Irish Minstrelsy*. How prettily the poem tells of its rise,

> Fed with a thousand invisible rills,
> Girdled around with the awe of the hills.

The next verse is worth quoting, for in it Miss Kavanagh seems to me to have reached a delicacy of expression and thought that reminds one of Kickham at his best. The lines, too, are full of that impassioned love for her country which was so deeply rooted in her heart:

Many a ruin, both abbey and cot,
Sees in your mirror a desolate lot.
Many an ear lying shut far away
Hearkened the tune that your dark ripples play.
One — I remember her better than all —
She knew every legend of cabin and hall;
Wept when the Law and the Famine-time met,
Sang how the Red Hand was radiantly set
Over the victors who fought at the Ford,
Over the sweep of O'Neill's Spanish sword —
O our own river! Where is she to-night?
Where are the exiles whose homes are in sight?

The last verse begins finely with

Once in the Maytime your carol so sweet
Found out my heart in the midst of the street;

and ends with a note of that tender sadness so very near to all she has written. Was it a shadow of the tomb?

A little westward of her home was Knockmany, celebrated by a wild, humorous tale of Carleton's, and not far off was the homestead where he himself was born and bred.

Miss Kavanagh came presently to Dublin, and studied art for a time at the Royal Dublin Society, but before long began to contribute articles and stories to the Dublin papers. When the Ladies' Land League had to find lady substitutes for imprisoned journalists, she took a prominent part. The Government even did her the honor to appoint a special detective to watch her. Strange Government to whom a bevy of young ladies was so awe inspiring! It must have been at this time, or just before it, that Miss Kavanagh inspired Kickham with his pleasant mock-serious little song, The Rose of Knockmany. When the Ladies' Land League had gone by, she contributed many short stories to Irish magazines, notably to the now extinct Irish Fireside, and for the last two or three years of her life managed the Uncle Remus Club for children, started by Mrs. Dwyer Gray in connection with The Irish Fireside, and continued in The Weekly Freeman.

In 1888 a number of her poems were included in *Poems and Ballads of Young Ireland*, a little volume which has had a sale sufficient at any rate to warrant its present new and cheaper form. It was planned out by a number of us, including Miss Rose Kavanagh, Miss Katharine Tynan, Miss Ellen O'Leary,

Dr. Todhunter and Dr. Douglas Hyde, the Gaelic scholar, with the aim, I hope not altogether unfulfilled, of adding another link, however small, to the long chain of Irish song that unites decade to decade. Every movement of Irish nationality has had its singers, and it seemed to us that our own times should not be dumb, even though the listeners were but few, and the singers' voices drowned in the roar of the market place. Miss Kavanagh's contributions were full of most delicate expression and tender music. At the time I often found myself repeating these lines from her Lough Bray:

> The amber ripples sang all day,
> And singing spilled their crowns of white
> Upon the beach, in thin pale spray
> That streaked the sober sand with light.

Perhaps, however, her most finished contribution was St. Michan's Churchyard. It is hardly needful to tell Irish readers that Emmet is supposed to be buried in St. Michan's Churchyard. The following are, I think, the best verses:

> Inside the city's throbbing heart
> One spot I know set well apart
> From life's hard highway, life's loud mart.

> A little, lonely, green graveyard,
> The old church tower its solemn guard,
> The gate with naught but sunbeams barred;

While other sunbeams went and came,
Above the stone which waits the name,
His land must write with Freedom's flame.

The slender elm above that stone,
Its summer wreath of leaves had thrown
Around the heart so quiet grown.

A robin, the bare boughs among,
Let loose his little soul in song —
Quick liquid gushes, fresh and strong!

And quiet heart, and bird, and tree,
Seemed linked in some strange sympathy
Too fine for mortal eye to see —

But full of balm and soothing sweet,
For those who sought that calm retreat;
For aching breast and weary feet.

The manner of such poetry much more closely resembles Kickham and Casey than Davis and Mangan. Like most of the best Irish verse of recent years it is meditative and sympathetic, rather than stirring and energetic: the trumpet has given way to the viol and the flute. It is easy to be unjust to such poetry, but very hard to write it. It springs straight out of the nature from some wellspring of refinement and gentleness. It makes half the pathos of literary history. When one reads some old poem of the sort one says: "What a charming mind had this writer! How gladly I should have met and talked with such a one!" and then one gathers about one, like a garment, the mist of regret.

For the last year or so Miss Kavanagh was able to do but little writing. Consumption was gradually doing its work. The winter of 1889 she spent in the south of France in a vain search for health. On her return to Ireland she went to live at her native village, where she died a few days ago. Her last poem was a memorial lyric prefixed to the poems of her friend, Miss Ellen O'Leary, who had herself addressed to Miss Kavanagh a little poem beginning:

> Brave eyes! brave eyes, how beautiful you are;
> Not dark as night, or gleaming like a star,
> But all alight with earnestness and truth,
> And the fond, foolish dreams of fervid youth.
>
> Brave eyes! brave eyes, and trustful too, as brave,
> In which thought follows thought, as wave on wave;
> True mirrors clear, reflecting every feeling,
> Now bright, now blank, now full of soft appealing.

April 11, 1891

THE POEMS OF ELLEN O'LEARY

Your Celt in London has been so busy about certain affairs of his own that he has let months go by without sending you any of his random notes, and let quite a pile of Irish books collect and lie unreviewed upon his table. Among those on which the dust lies least thickly — for it is among the last arrivals — is *Lays of Country*, *Home and Friends*, a little green book of poems by Miss Ellen O'Leary. She was able to partly correct the proofs, but did not live to look on the completed book; our Irish printers — or whoever was responsible — have been laggards indeed. If I remember rightly, Mr. Rolleston's introduction was written and in proof almost, if not quite, two years ago. However, it is a book worth waiting for. I am distinctly of the opinion that Miss O'Leary was a better writer than either "Mary" or "Eva" of The Nation. She had not the good fortune to live in a period when all Ireland was supremely interested in songs and ballads, when The Nation newspaper was filling the four corners of the land with lay and lyric. Had she done so, her name would long ago have been as well known as theirs. As it is, no maker of Irish anthologies will neglect this little green book. The following is a song in the old sense of the word, that is to say, a singable poem worthy of good music. The compilers of our songbooks, ballad sheets and the like, should garner it:

I sit beside my darling's grave,
  Who in the prison died,
And tho' my tears fall thick and fast,
  I think of him with pride:
Ay, softly fall my tears like dew,
For one to God and Ireland true.

"I love my God o'er all," he said,
  "And then I love my land,
And next I love my Lily sweet,
  Who pledged me her white hand:
To each — to all — I'm ever true,
To God — to Ireland — and to you."

No tender nurse his hard bed smoothed
  Or softly raised his head;
He fell asleep and woke in heaven
  Ere I knew he was dead;
Yet why should I my darling rue?
He was to God and Ireland true.

Oh! 'tis a glorious memory,
  I'm prouder than a queen
To sit beside my hero's grave
  And think on what has been:
And, oh, my darling, I am true
To God — to Ireland — and to you.

The Emigrant's Return, A Voice, Home to
Carriglea, A Legend of Tyrone, Ireland's
Dead, and My Own Galtees are favorites of
mine and will, I believe, drift into our song
and ballad books. They are all written according to the Davis tradition, rather than the
more elaborate one of Moore and his imita-
tors. Nothing could be more simple, nothing

more sincere. The book has for frontispiece a good photograph of the author, and is introduced by Mr. T. W. Rolleston, who describes Miss O'Leary's connection with the Fenian movement, and by Sir Charles Gavan Duffy, who writes six pages of criticisms of the poems.

Two books that have been lying on my table several weeks are *Poems*, by John Francis O'Donnell, and *Whisper!* by Miss Wynne. They differ in every way from the simple ballads I have just been noticing. They are elaborate, ornate and literary, and show a strong influence from English writers. The Southwark Irish Literary Club, who at great labor have gathered together O'Donnell's poems from old magazines and newspapers, must forgive my bracketing their bulky volume with Miss Wynne's little venture. I know quite well that O'Donnell has stood the test of time to some extent, for he died as long ago as 1874, and that Miss Wynne is but a writer of pretty, skilful and rather trivial little verses. They both, however, belong to the same school of Irish writers. Both have read much English literature, and have taken from it, rather than from their own minds and the traditions of their own country, the manner and matter of their poetry. They have left behind them the simple national ballad manner, without proving strong enough to reach that more ample and subtle style the greatest writers learn, in part, from knowing and modelling themselves upon the best masters of verse and prose in every country of the world. To criticise Miss Wynne in this fashion is certainly rather like breaking a butterfly on a wheel; but O'Donnell had so much gift for expression that he might have achieved a style in happier circumstances. A notion of what he might have done may be gathered from the following opening to an ode on The Four Masters:

Where sleep the Four? What blessed earth —
What aisles, with burning windows, hold
In porphyry, or red rough gold,
The sages of the South and North?
Where rest the men who, whilst this Isle
Was barred with black oppression's cloud,
Faced death and dungeons with a smile,
Nor held their heads less straight and proud?
They crept to peace in far Louvain,
Shrouded in the Franciscan grain:
Caring no more to greet the sun,
The hand's work and the heart's work done.

Beside the sea of Donegal —
The coasts beloved of Gaul and Spain —
From sunrise to the sunset's wane,
Their shadows dropped from wall to wall
Through years of change. Few watched their toil,
And fewer still the glory prized

Of saving from a trampled spoil
  The truths a warring world despised:
There in that narrow little room,
Our martyrs' palms took fresher bloom,
And o'er those rudely sanded floors
Moved poets, kings and warriors.

Here is fulness of music and richness of
phrase — despite a commonplace metaphor
here and there like that about "oppression's
cloud"; but as the ode goes on, it becomes
monotonous and shows, like most of his work,
frequent Tennysonian mannerisms that spoil
its originality. With more leisure or more culture, O'Donnell might have discovered a style
quite his own. As it was, he was stifled by
journalism. "Talking of work," he wrote in
1872, "since Sunday, two columns of notes,
two columns of London gossip, and a leader,
one column, and two columns of verse for
The Nation. For Catholic Opinion, two pages
of notes and a leader. For Illustrated Magazine, three poems and five columns of story."
A style is not picked up in this fashion. A
career of this kind for a man of imagination,
if voluntary, is a crime; if involuntary, the
greatest of misfortunes; and yet O'Donnell
seems to have been rather proud of it. "I
write verse faster than prose," he said. Oh
thou great abyss of inane facility, how many
fine natures hast thou swallowed — above all,

how many Celtic ones? An unkind Providence has granted to us Irish folk a terrible love of immediate results, wholly fatal to great work. It will leave us with the approach of more orderly and successful times. We shall learn then to trust the future sufficiently to work for it. At present three sentences of mingled admiration and blame, which I heard the wittiest Irishman of our day apply to his countrymen, are in some manner true. "We are," he said, "too poetical to be poets [great ones, he meant]. We are the greatest talkers since the Greeks. We are a nation of brilliant failures." A love for immediate results makes us pour out our faculties on the mere arts of life. Hence, perhaps, our humor and that charm our bitterest enemies — Mr. Froude, for instance — are so ready to find in Irish character; but hence, too, the absence of any very great epic and ample modern Irish book or poem. We will change all that when prosperity has taught us to trust in the morrow, and live for it. The Celt has done great works in the past — witness *The Tain Bo* and all that hoard of epic tales — and will, beyond question, do great works in the future. Meanwhile he has created a modern ballad literature, no common feat in these sophisticated times.

I find some token of a new state of things,

such as I have foretold, in the fourth book
that awaits mention. It is the last arrival, has
only lain for about a month atop of O'Donnell's poems, waiting the writing of this letter.
It is a collection of folk tales under the name
of *Beside the Fire*, partly new and partly long
expected translations of a portion of the
Leabhar Sgeulaighteachta, as Dr. Hyde has
named his book of Gaelic stories. If Dr. Hyde
carries out his intentions, and continues to
gather and write out, in that perfect style of
his, traditions, legends and old rhymes, he
will give the world one of those monumental
works whose absence from modern Irish literature I have been lamenting. We have had
Gaelic scholars of great learning, but none
who have had the literary culture of Mr.
Hyde. He has both knowledge and imagination, a somewhat rare combination, and I
think he may be set down as the coming man
in Gaelic scholarship. His name is gradually
spreading beyond the four seas of Ireland. An
English authority of note said to me a while
since, when speaking of Dr. Hyde's telling of
a particular legend, "There never was such a
folk-lorist." Certainly, at any rate, we have
never had such a one, and if he makes his
work as exhaustive as it is fine, no country of
the world will have seen his master.

I may mention among forthcoming books an Irish historical romance by the younger Standish O'Grady. It deals with the Tyrone rebellion and the battle of Kinsale. Your Celt in London vows some day to give it a whole column, if he can run so large a cargo across the harbor bar of editorial watchfulness.

April 18, 1891

THE POISON FLOWER

Dr. Todhunter is known, or should be, to Irish people for his volume of Irish poems with its charming versions of The Children of Lir and The Sons of Turann, but to the London public he is best known for his plays. *Helena in Troas*, when acted four or five years ago, was an immense success. It not merely drew the cultivated public who care for poetry or for Greek drama, but filled the theatre with the ordinary run of theatre-goers. It was such a success, indeed, that several hundreds of pounds were taken at the first performance alone.

Much of this was doubtless due to the wonderful stage — the only exact reproduction of the stage of ancient Athens seen in the modern world — and to the no less wonderful stage management of E. W. Godwin. Modern play-goers do not greatly care for poetry when it comes with no recommendation besides itself, but are ready enough to tolerate and, per-haps, even enjoy it, when they are lifted out of what Shelley called "the trance of real life" by beautiful and strange surroundings. Hence they admired *Helena*, as before that they had admired the performance of Fletch-er's *Faithful Shepherdess*, when acted in the open air at Combe by Lady Archibald Camp-bell's pastoral players. There is a small, per-haps growing, public that does indeed care for poetry for its own sake, but it in no way re-sembles the great public of the theatres. Dr. Todhunter's *Sicilian Idyll*, when acted at Bedford Park last year, won the applause of this small body. For six or seven nights it filled the little theatre — a pleasant sight for all who hope to see true literary drama once more.

Now, however, Dr. Todhunter has tried to reach the common run of playgoers once more. Last week he revived the *Idyll* at the Vaude-ville, and preluded it with a new play founded on Hawthorne's Rappaccini's Daughter, and called *The Poison Flower*. The small public who love poetry was there, and enthusiastic, and the larger public came also, but not in great numbers, and showed by the comments I could overhear how strange a thing poetry and romance have come to be in its ears, when not sanctioned by long usage, as is the case with Shakespeare, or made to seem possible by surroundings strange enough to break "the trance of real life."

Both the *Idyll* and *The Poison Flower* are much more dramatic than *Helena in Troas*, and lacked only its solemn staging, its rhythmic chorus and its ascending incense to move the audience much more powerfully. As it was, people needed, coming in fresh from the trivialities of the world of shops and tea tables, the "once upon a time" that begins the make believe of fairy tales. Many people have said to me that the surroundings of *Helena* made them feel religious. Once get your audience in that mood, and you can do anything with it.

I described *A Sicilian Idyll* to you at the time of its first performance, and so need only speak now of *The Poison Flower*. Dr. Todhunter has taken the story of the young girl who grew up among the poisoned flowers of the magician's garden until she, too, was poisonous as the flowers themselves, and added to it some hint of mystical significance, no less than much secondary incident. The story, as it is told in *Mosses from an Old Manse*, beautiful as it is, has always seemed to me a little fanciful and arbitrary. I never quite could get it out of my head that Hawthorne wanted to make one's flesh creep like the little boy in *A Winter's Tale*, and did not much care how he managed it. In the play it becomes a much more solid thing. One finds it quite easy to believe that this worn-looking Kabalist, who crosses the stage with cat-like tread, has in his mind some wild dream for the regeneration of men, and that he is bringing up in the garden, whose strange and exotic flowers rise before one, a new Eve to be mother of a new race to whom the poisons of the world — its diseases and crimes — shall do no hurt, for they will carry within themselves "the poison that drives out poison." The copy of the Kabala that lies upon my own desk pleads for him, and tells us that such men lived, and may well have dreamed just such a dream, in the mystic Middle Ages. In becoming a thinker of a particular school, he has obtained the historical reality lacked by the Rappaccini of Hawthorne; and by the occult intention of his experiment being explained to us he has been united to many men in many ages. Even in our own day men

dream of "the poison that drives out poison." Witness the recent rumor that some
modern but still Italian Rappaccini had discovered the bacillus of old age.

I hear some talk of the play being put on in
America. It might prosper with you. Browning — I do not think any of his recent biographers have mentioned it — got three hundred
and fifty dollars from the American revival of
A Blot in the 'Scutcheon; not a large sum, but
certainly more than it ever fetched in England. You seem, indeed, to have much more
liking for the verse drama than people have
this side of the water. Dr. Todhunter's play
does not pretend to be great poetry, but it is
charming, romantic and interesting, and may
please some portion of the many with you as
ardently as it has pleased the few with us.
You, however, will not have the chance of seeing the charming actress Dr. Todhunter has
discovered and written the part of heroine for.
Her performance of Beatrice, the girl who
lived among the poisoned flowers, was as intense and passionate as her rendering of the
rôle of Amaryllis, in the *Idyll*, was graceful
and self-contained. She made her first appearance in any important part on the Bedford Park stage, but has since then become
well known to theatre-goers through her act-

ing in Ibsen's *Rosmerholm*. She will always, however, be best, I believe, in poetic drama, her exquisite recitation being no small part of her charm.

August 1, 1891

A BALLAD SINGER

I DO not head this letter The Celt in London as my wont is, for I am back in Ireland for the time being, and writing out on the lawn of an old Irish thatched farmhouse. An apple tree covered with red apples shakes softly before me in the sunlight, and the paper on which I write rests on the stone top of a sundial. Behind me in the hedge a grasshopper has just lifted his shrill song. To talk of books at all on this green clover spotted grass seems sadly out of keeping, unless, indeed, it be some dreamy romance like *Marius the Epicurean*, whose golden sentences, laden as with sleepy sunlight, I have been reading slowly and fitfully since morning, taking the book up for a moment and then laying it down again, and letting my mind stray off to the red apples and the shadowing leaves before me.

But then *Marius the Epicurean* is not writ in my bond. With Irish literature and Irish

thought alone have I to do. And yet the doctrines I have just been studying in Pater's
jewelled paragraphs — the Platonic theory
of spiritual beings having their abode in all
things without and within us, and thus
uniting all things, as by a living ladder of
souls, with God Himself — have some relation
to those very matters of Irish thought that
bring me to Ireland just now.

I am here looking for stories of the fairies
and the phantoms, and are not these spiritual
beings of Plato but the phantoms and fairies
of philosophy? I have been away in County
Down, looking almost in vain among its half-
Scotch people for the legends I find so plenti-
ful in the West. I heard, indeed, of two people
who are said to have been killed by the fairies
for taking up fairy thorn trees, in the last
eight months, and of certain phantoms living
among the marshes, but got no legends of any
interest; and now I am faring somewhat better
here in County Dublin. A few minutes ago,
an old woman came out of the kitchen and
went into the yard, which I can see from my
seat by the sundial, and fed some chickens.
In her childhood she was fairy-struck (she insists) on a fairy rath, and made ill for months.
Yet people tell me that the belief in fairies is
gone. Ah, no! There are still stories told with

most entire faith in every quiet county bar-
ony. In the towns the fairy tradition is gone
indeed, but even there the supernatural sur-
vives in visions and ghost-hauntings.

I was the other day sitting reading on the
steps of the country house in Down where I
was staying, when a ballad singer came up the
avenue with his little fluttering strips of paper
flying in the wind, and asked me would I like
to hear an old Waterloo man sing a song. The
man was clearly a liar, as he could not be
more than forty or forty-five years old at
most; but none the less I listened to him, and
bought some of his ballad sheets. The verses
proved to be mainly rubbish of the usual kind,
but there was among them one poem of great
beauty. I at first thought it must be a reprint
from some of our Irish poets; but then I do
not remember having read it, and I know our
Irish poets pretty thoroughly. It must, after
all, be, I think, a genuine street ballad. Here
are three of the verses:

> I'll sing to-night of that fairy land
>   In the lap of the ocean set,
> And of all the lands I have travelled o'er
>   It's the loveliest I have met;
> Where the willows weep and the roses sleep,
>   And the balmy breezes blow,
> For that dear old land, that sweet old land,
>   Where the ancient shamrocks grow.

I'll sing of that lovely old churchyard,
  Where my father's bones are laid,
In clusters stand those ruins grand
  Which tyrant foes have made;
And I'll strike the harp with a mournful touch,
  While the glistening tears will flow,
For that dear old land, that sweet old land,
  Where the ancient shamrocks grow.

I'll sing of Ireland's ancient days,
  When our sires were kingly men,
Who led the chase and manly race
  Through forest, field and glen;
Whose only word was the shining sword,
  And their pen — the patriot's blow!
For that dear old land, that sweet old land,
  Where the ancient shamrocks grow.

What infinite sadness there is in these verses! What wild beauty! The man when he sold them to me did so timidly, mistaking me, most evidently, for one of the loyal minority. "There is a deal of liberality in them," he said, in quaint apology.

The song about The Ancient Shamrocks is the best piece of Irish literature I have met since I came to Ireland; much better in every way, it certainly is, than this new Irish magazine — The Irish Monthly Illustrated Journal — lying in its yellow cover across the blue shadow of the dial before me. The thing is well written enough, but what in the name of goodness has an Irish magazine to do with

Mr. Stead and the German Emperor? If people want to know about either, they will go to the English periodicals. An Irish magazine should give us Irish subjects. Have we no Irish sins to denounce, no Irish virtues to encourage, no Irish legends to record, no Irish stories to tell, that we must sing the praises of the Emperor of Germany and Mr. Stead, both of them gentlemen who have no need of a trumpeter? Why should we feebly imitate the methods and matter of English magazines? At the same time I am very glad to see this new monthly, especially as it is not all given up to foreign subject matter, but does make some slight reference to Dublin men and Dublin things. It has a very clever editor in Mr. Eyre, and it may not be his fault that it is not more Irish. I do not know what difficulties in the way of want of pence he, like most Irish editors, has to contend against.

When I say that The Ancient Shamrocks is the best thing I have seen this side of the water, I do not mean to belittle Miss Katharine Tynan's *A Nun, Her Friends and Her Order*. I saw it before I left the other side. It is very picturesque and charming, and brings the nunnery life most vividly before the eyes of the reader. Well written as it is, however, it cannot compete with Miss Tynan's verse.

Her new book of poems, the contents of which I have seen, will, I feel certain, give her a higher position than anything she has yet done. It will quite overshadow this *Nun, Her Friends and Her Order*; and yet the *Nun* is a good book, and I would say much more about it were I not somewhat astray among those saints and holy people. Besides, the grasshoppers have begun to chant in the hedge once more. I listen to them and let all books and bookish things die away out of my mind. What do they sing of so gaily? They were singing before Troy was built, or seven-gated Thebes repelled the encompassing armies; Socrates heard them on the banks of the Ilissus; and still they sing on as of old. What do they sing of? Of the loves and wars of grasshoppers, and of the joy of men living in the sunlight. I will put aside my pen and paper and let my mind, listening to their song, go away and dream among the green shadows and red apples.

September 12, 1891

THE RHYMERS' CLUB

In France literature divides itself into schools, movements and circles. At one moment the Decadents, at another the Symbolists, to-day the Parnassians, tomorrow the Naturalists, hold the public ear and win acceptance for their theory and practice of literature. In England the writers do not form groups, but each man works by himself and for himself, for England is the land of literary Ishmaels. It is only among the sociable Celtic nations that men draw nearer to each other when they want to think and dream and work. All this makes the existence of the Rhymers' Club the more remarkable a thing. Into this little body, as about a round table of rhyme, have gathered well nigh all the poets of the new generation who have public enough to get their works printed at the cost of the publisher, and some not less excellent, who cannot yet mount that first step of the ladder famewards. Not that the Rhymers' Club is a school of poets in the French sense, for the writers who belong to it resemble each other in but one thing: they all believe that the deluge of triolets and rondeaus has passed away, and that we must look once more upon the world with serious eyes and set to music — each according to his lights — the deep soul of humanity. "What is the good of writing poetry at all now?" said the other day a noted verse writer whose fame was at its height ten years ago. "Sonnets are played

out and ballades and rondeaus are no longer
novel, and nobody has invented a new form."
All, despairing, cry of the departing age, but
the world still goes on, and the soul of man is
ever young, and its song shall never come to
an end. The names of some few of the Rhymers may have already been blown across the
Atlantic, though more probably they have
not, for all but one are of the very newest literary generation. There is Arthur Symons,
who has made the music halls of London and
Paris his peculiar study, and set forth their
gaieties and tragedies in even, deftest verse,
and John Davidson, who has just published a
series of poems on a Scotch music hall. In
both writers one finds that search for new subject matter, new emotions, which so clearly
marks the reaction from that search for new
forms merely, which distinguished the generation now going out. "He is no poet who would
not go to Japan for a new form," wrote a distinguished member of the Gosse, Lang and
Dobson school.

Arthur Symons is a scholar in music halls
as another man might be a Greek scholar or
an authority on the age of Chaucer. He has
studied them for purposes of literature and
remained himself, if I understand him rightly,
quite apart from their glitter and din. He has

gone to travel among them as another man
might go to travel in Persia, and has done it
thoroughly, being familiar with those of many
cities. John Davidson, upon the other hand,
claims to have lived his verses. In the Pro-
logue to his just published *In a Music Hall*,
one reads:

> I did as my desk-fellows did;
> With a pipe and a tankard of beer,
> In a music-hall, rancid and hot,
> I lost my soul night after night.
> It is better to lose one's soul,
> Than never to stake it at all.

No two attitudes towards the world and literature could be more different, and despite
the community of subject no two styles could
be more dissimilar than those of John Davidson and Arthur Symons. One has more fire
and enthusiasm, and the other more art and
subtlety. Fine as much (notably the haunting and wonderful Selene Eden) certainly is,
I find my enjoyment checked continually by
some crudity of phrase. The din and glitter
one feels were far too near the writer. He has
not been able to cast them back in imaginative
dimness and distance. Of Mr. Symons'
method I will speak at length when his book
comes to me. I have but seen stray poems
and judge from them that, despite most
manifest triumphs from time to time, he will

sometimes fail through gaining too easily that very dimness and distance I have spoken of. He will, perhaps, prove to be too far from, as Mr. Davidson is too near to, his subject. I must say that the author of *In a Music Hall* is entirely successful in some of the romantic poems that follow the *Music Hall* verses. Notable is that radiant poem in which the gleeman tells how

> Starry truth
> Still maintains a changing strife
> With the purple dreams of youth;

and notable also are For Lovers, and parts of Anselm and Bianca.

Both writers are, whether they succeed or fail, interesting signs of the times. Not merely are they examples of that desire for new subject matter of which I have spoken, but of the reaction from the super-refinement of much recent life and poetry. The cultivated man has begun a somewhat hectic search for the common pleasures of common men and for the rough accidents of life. The typical young poet of our day is an aesthete with a surfeit, searching sadly for his lost Philistinism, his heart full of an unsatisfied hunger for the commonplace. He is an Alastor tired of his woods and longing for beer and skittles.

The most like Alastor in appearance among

the Rhymers is certainly Richard Le Gallienne. The Review of Reviews has made
many familiar with his refined Shelley-like
face, and his own *Book Bills of Narcissus* —
a half romance, half autobiography — with
his moods and his history. The longing for
Philistine beer and skittles has perhaps beset
him less ardently than the bulk of his fellows,
and he still prides himself on wearing the am-
brosial locks of the poet. The longing for a
new subject has filled him as full as his neighbors, however, and has led him to publish a
book of poems, *Volumes in Folio*, which has
dealt with nothing in the world but the buy-
ing and treasuring of rare books. A very
pleasant glamour of Keats-like romance did
he weave about them, too. But *Volumes in
Folio* is ancient history, and I have to do but
with the present and the future. Lionel Johnson, who has somewhere about him a long
poem called Gloria Mundi, full of Catholic
theology, and George Greene, who is writing
a whole book of verse on the *Inferno* of Dante,
are other typical members. Ernest Rhys, of
Camelot fame, and T. W. Rolleston are constant frequenters. I need not multiply names.
They will all be on the title page of the forthcoming *Book of the Rhymers' Club*, the mani-
festo of the circle.

I said that all, with one exception, belong to the newest literary generation. That exception is important, for it is Dr. Todhunter, who has just published a shilling edition of his book of Irish poems, and so concerns us more than all the others. If we do not take care of our own singers, who will? The book is called *The Banshee* and is sold by Sealy, Bryers & Walker, Middle Abbey Street, Dublin. I need not say much now about it, for it was reviewed enthusiastically and fully by all the Irish-American papers on its first appearance a couple of years ago. In it Dr. Todhunter follows in the footsteps of Sir Samuel Ferguson and gives us simple and stately versions of The Children of Lir and Sons of Turann. There is no better way of getting a knowledge of two of the most lovely of all the old Irish stories than from this book. May many follow in the road Dr. Todhunter has chosen. It leads where there is no lack of subjects, for the literature of Ireland is still young, and on all sides of this road is Celtic tradition and Celtic passion crying for singers to give them voice. England is old and her poets must scrape up the crumbs of an almost finished banquet, but Ireland has still full tables.

April 23, 1892

MAUDE GONNE

ENGLAND has indeed, as Mitchel phrased it, gained the ear of the world, and knows right well how to tell foreign nations what tale of Ireland pleases her best. By the mouths of her magnificent Times, and her countless tourists and sight-seers even from the wealthier and more conservative classes, she repeats to the admiring nations a ceaseless tale of English patience and Irish insubordination. More than one Irishman has sought in vain to get a hearing for some Irish thoughts on the matter. The late Mr. Leonard tried all his life to make the people of Paris listen to the true story of England and Ireland, and with no very noticeable success. But now Miss Maud Gonne, as eloquent with her tongue as was "Speranza" with her pen, has made her voice heard where so many have failed. Every speech has been a triumph, and every triumph greater than the one that went before it. Thousands who come to see this new wonder — a beautiful woman who makes speeches — remain to listen with delight to her sincere and simple eloquence. Last week at Bordeaux, an audience of twelve hundred persons rose to its feet, when she had finished, to applaud her with wild enthusiasm. The papers of Russia, France, Germany and even Egypt quote her speeches, and the tale of Irish wrongs has found its way hither and thither to lie stored up, perhaps, in many a memory against the day of need. She is going through France addressing town after town, and beside spreading a better knowledge of Ireland and awakening a wider sympathy with our wrongs, has already, though this is not her main object, gained, I believe, a considerable sum for the evicted tenants.

It is not, however, to describe her success that I write, but to review a supplement to La Revue Catholique which has just reached me. It is a verbatim report of her long speech at the Catholic University of the Luxembourg, and enables one to judge once for all whether she rule her audiences by the power of beauty alone, or whether she have indeed the genius of the orator. I do not think that any one who reads through these twelve columns of clear and vigorous French will doubt the answer. I have heard many lady speakers, some of them being the most celebrated of their class, but do not remember finding in any of their words the same kind of faculty I find in these columns of La Revue Catholique. Miss Gonne is the first who has spoken on the platform wholly and undisguisedly out of a woman's heart. The speeches of the others might have been made by men, but this speech, while never weak, never sentimental in the bad sense of the word, is the kind of speech, both in its limitations and in its triumphs, which could only be made by a woman. From first to last it is emotional and even poignant, and has that curious power of unconsciously seizing salient incidents which is so distinguishing a mark of the novel writing of women. Its logic is none the less irresistible because it is the logic of the heart. Listen to her description of the famine of '48:

The Middle Ages in the most sombre period of their history never beheld such misery. Men and women ate the dogs, the rats, and the grass of the field, and some even, when all food was gone, ate the dead bodies. Those who died were cast into great ditches so hurriedly opened and badly closed again that the pestilential odors helped to make death travel more rapidly. They were called the pits of the famine, for into them the famine cast all its harvest. Ireland was heroic in her suffering. Whole families, when they had eaten their last crust, and understood that they had to die, looked once upon the sun and then closed up the doors of their cabins with stones, that no one might look on their last agony. Weeks afterwards men would find their skeletons gathered round the extinguished hearth. I do not exaggerate, gentlemen. I have added nothing to the mournful reality. If you come to my country, every stone will repeat to you this tragic history. It was only fifty years ago. It still lives in thousands of memories. I have been told it by women who have heard the last sigh of their children without being able to lessen their agony with one drop of milk. It has seemed to me at evening on those mountains of Ireland, so full of savage majesty when the wind sighed over the pits of the famine where the thousands of dead enrich the harvests of the future, it has seemed to me that I heard an avenging voice calling down on our oppressors the execration of men and the justice of God.

The bulk of the spoken oratory of our time has, like the whole of our spoken drama, divorced itself from literature, but this passage has much of the serene beauty of good writing. Nor has it lost in gaining this any of its effectiveness as an oratorical appeal, for with rare mastery over the picturesque it unrolls incidents that compel attention and burn themselves into the memory. A man or woman trained on the political platforms of the day would have given figures and arguments and have been forgotten ten minutes after. But many who heard this passage will never forget as long as they live the skeletons huddled by the extinguished hearths and the great pits where lie thousands who make fertile the harvests of the future. Perhaps, too, some will remember the voice calling upon the

mountain at evening, and if the need come, be
ready in our service.

The whole speech shows this power of seizing upon the distinguishing incidents of an
epoch and describing them in vivid and living
sentences. It was no easy thing to give a clear
picture of the history of Ireland in a speech of
three-quarters of an hour, or an hour at most,
without needless digression on the one hand
or dry catalogues of events upon the other;
yet this is what Miss Gonne has done with
such perfect success. She takes her audience
from incident to incident, from the bloodless
conversion of pagan Ireland through the very
bloody battle when hoariest Brian died in the
moment of victory to the English invasion
and down to our own day and the death of
Parnell, and every event is described as vividly and simply as if it were all in some famous
ballad of "old, unhappy, far-off things, and
battles long ago."

July 30, 1892

THE IRISH NATIONAL LITERARY
SOCIETY

YOUR Celt has written the greater bulk of his
letters from the capitol of the enemy, but he
is now among his own people again, and no

longer The Celt in London, but The Celt in Ireland. At this moment he is sitting writing, or trying to write, in the big, florid new National Library with its stone balcony, where nobody is allowed to walk, and its numberless stone niches, in which there will never be any statues. He is sitting dreaming much, and writing a little from time to time, watching the people come and go, and wondering what shall be born of the new generation that is now so very busy reading endless scholasticisms along the five rows of oak tables. An old fairy tale which exists in many forms in many countries tells of a giant whose life was hidden away in an egg, which was in its turn hid in the mouth of a fish, or some such unlikely place. The library is just such an egg, for it hides under its white curved ceiling a good portion of the scholastic life of student Dublin. Here they come to read for examinations, and to work up their various subjects. At my left hand is a man reading some registers of civil service or other examinations; opposite me an ungainly young man with a puzzled face is turning over the pages of a trigonometry work; and a little beyond him a medical student is deep in anatomical diagrams. On all sides men are studying the things that are to get them bodily food, but no man among them is searching for the imaginative and spiritual food to be got out of great literature. Nobody, with the exception of a few ladies, perhaps, ever seems to do any disinterested reading in this library, or indeed anywhere else in Ireland. Every man here is grinding at the mill wherein he grinds all things into pounds and shillings, and but few of them will he get when all is done. Ireland, half through her own fault and half through circumstances over which she has no control, is not a reading nation, nor has she been so for many a long day. A single town in Scotland is said to buy more books than all Ireland put together, and surely nowhere out of Ireland will you find a great library like this given over completely to the student cramming for examinations.

Can we find a remedy? Can we not unite literature to the great passion of patriotism and ennoble both thereby? This question has occupied a good many of us this spring. We think that a national literary society and a series of national books like Duffy's Library of Ireland may do something, and have accordingly founded such a society and planned out, with the help of a number of well known men of letters, such a national series. Our task should not, after all, be so difficult. These very students will do for the love of Ireland what they would not do for the love of literature. When literature comes to them, telling of their own country and of its history and of its legends, they will listen gladly enough. The people of Ireland have ever honored intellect, although they have no intellectual life themselves. I have heard a drunken fisherman tell a man that he was no gentleman "because nobody is a gentleman who has not been educated at Trinity College, Dublin." The people of Ireland have created perhaps the most beautiful folk-lore in the world, and have made a wild music that is the wonder of all men, and yet to-day they have turned aside from imaginative arts. Can we bring them to care once more for the things of the mind? Well, we are going to do our best to bring books to their doors and music, too, perhaps. Thomas of Erceldoune foretold the day when the gray goose quill would rule the world; and may not we men of the pen hope to move some Irish hearts and make them beat true to manhood and to Ireland? Will not the day come when we shall have again in Ireland men who will not lie for any party advantage, or traffic away eternal principles for any expediency however urgent — men like the men of '48, who lived by the light of noble books and the great traditions of the past? Amidst the clash of party against party we have tried to put forward a nationality that is above party, and amid the oncoming roar of a general election we have tried to assert those everlasting principles of love of truth and love of country that speak to men in solitude and in the silence of the night. So far all has gone well with us, for men who are saddened and disgusted with the turn public affairs have taken have sought in our society occasion to do work for Ireland that will bring about assured good, whether that good be great or small. We have met more support than we ventured to hope for, and there is no sign of its falling off.

The committee represents all parties and opinions which have any claim to be considered national. The Reverend T. A. Finlay of the Catholic University, Mr. John O'Leary, Sir Charles Gavan Duffy, Dr. Douglas Hyde, Dr. Sigerson, Count Plunkett, Miss Katharine Tynan, Miss Maud Gonne, so well known for her oratory and her beauty, and Mr. Richard Ashe King, the novelist, are among the best known. Books have been offered upon all manner of national epochs and events from the Ossianic days to our own time.

Apart from the literary society altogether, things are not looking so badly for the future of our literature. Mr. Standish O'Grady, for instance, is doing better and better work. He has on hand an historical romance dealing with the invasions of Strongbow, and is contributing also from time to time singularly moving and picturesque little stories on events in Irish history to the Dublin papers. He will doubtless collect them into a volume before long. He has also written for Fisher Unwin's Children's Library a book called *Finn and His Companions*, which gives the most vivid pictures of the Ossianic age I ever hope to see. Caoilte, having survived to the time of St. Patrick by enchantment, describes to the saint the life of the Fenians, and tells numbers of the old tales out of the bardic poems in English both powerful and beautiful.

Dr. Douglas Hyde has also a book on the legendary age in progress. It will give translations of bardic stories, and will be, I believe, but the first of a series if Dr. Hyde meets with proper support. It is impossible to overrate the importance of such books, for in them the Irish poets of the future will in all likelihood find a good portion of their subject matter. From that great candle of the past we must all light our little tapers.

In England I sometimes hear men complain that the old themes of verse and prose are used up. Here in Ireland the marble block is waiting for us almost untouched, and the statues will come as soon as we have learned to use the chisel. Our history is full of incidents well worthy of drama, story and song. And they are incidents involving types of character of which this world has not yet heard. If we can but put those tumultuous centuries into tale or drama, the whole world will listen to us and sit at our feet like children who hear a new story. Nor is this new thing we have to say in our past alone. The very people who come and go in this library where I write are themes full of new wisdom and new mystery, for in them is that yet uncultured thing — Irish character. And if history and the living present fail us, do there not lie hid among those spear heads and golden collars over the way in the New Museum, suggestions of that age before history when the art legends and wild mythology of earliest Ireland rose out of the void? There alone is enough of the stuff that dreams are made on to keep us busy a thousand years.

November 19, 1892

FROM THE PROVIDENCE
SUNDAY JOURNAL

THE POET
OF BALLYSHANNON *

IN THIS age of ambitious thoughts, this cosmopolitan age, when poets have ransacked
the world for their themes, the author of this
little volume has sung for the most part his
own countryside and his seaboard towns:

> A wild west Coast, a little Town,
> Where little Folk go up and down,
> Tides flow and winds blow:
> Night and Tempest and the Sea,
> Human Will and Human Fate:
> What is little, what is great?
> Howsoe'er the answer be,
> Let me sing of what I know.

In many more verses, beautiful as these, he
has sung it. To be read in this age you must
have ambitious thoughts, offer some solution
of the old riddle. You must draw heaven and
earth into your net. That is as it should be,
perhaps. It is certainly as it must be. It is
possible we shall some day discover that these
nineteenth century thoughts of ours are only
bubble thoughts. But meanwhile we have so
many things on our hands, so much to break
and make, we can hardly listen at all to one
who turning aside sings the folk-lore and

* Irish Songs and Poems. By William Allingham. London, 1887.

memories of a little seaboard town. We —
we are of the age. The spirit of the age has
never been heard of down there. In their old
crannie they still believe in spirits and fairies
and ghosts. Hence has it come about, this
poet of Ballyshannon has found few readers.
Children have loved him. They are always of
the past ages — they and the very old. If
they are wise children, to them it is of more
importance to know that ghosts and fairies
are not on speaking terms than to have at
your finger ends all notions that ever were
cradled in lecture rooms:

> The Moon was bright, the Sea was still,
> The Fairies danced on Fairy Hill;
> The Town lay sleeping far below;
> Ghosts went round it, sad and slow,
> Loth to leave their earthly place
> For the Wilderness of Space.
> The watch-dogs saw the Ghosts and howl'd,
> The Fairies saw the Ghosts, and cowl'd
> Their little heads and whirl'd away;
> No friendship between Ghost and Fay.
> Fairies lightly love Mankind,
> To mischief or to mirth inclined,
> They fear the Dead, by night or day.

Perhaps, also, to fully understand these
poems one needs to have been born and bred
in one of those western Irish towns; to remember how it was the centre of your world,
how the mountains and the river and the

roads became a portion of your life forever;
to have loved with a sense of possession even
the roadside bushes where the roadside cot-
tagers hung their clothes to dry. That sense
of possession was the very centre of the matter. Elsewhere you are only a passer-by, for
everything is owned by so many that it is
owned by no one. Down there as you hummed
over Allingham's Fairies and looked up at the
mountain where they lived, it seemed to you
that a portion of your life was the subject.
How much, too, did it not add to remember
that old Biddy So-and-So, at the river's side,
laid milk and bread outside her door every
evening to wheedle into prosperity-giving
humor those same fairies of the song:

> Up the airy mountain,
>   Down the rushy glen,
> We daren't go a-hunting
>   For fear of little men;
> Wee folk, good folk,
>   Trooping all together;
> Green jacket, red cap,
>   And white owl's feather!
>
> Down along the rocky shore
>   Some make their home,
> They live on crispy pancakes
>   Of yellow tide-foam;
> Some in the reeds
>   Of the black mountain lake,
> With frogs for their watch-dogs,
>   All night awake.

> High on the hill-top
>   The old King sits;
> He is now so old and gray
>   He's nigh lost his wits.
> With a bridge of white mist
>   Columbkill he crosses,
> On his stately journeys
>   From Slieveleague to Rosses.

And so on — such songs, the heart covers them with its ivy.

Many more such local themes are there in this last book of the poet of Ballyshannon: the pilot's daughter in her Sunday frock — the wake with the candles round the corpse and a cloth under the chin — the ruined Abbey of Asaroe, an old man who was of the blood of those who founded it, watching sadly the crumbled walls — girls sewing and singing under a thorn tree — the piano from some larger house, a jumble of old memories! Memories, be it noticed, of things and moments, more than of passions and persons. Everywhere the little hooks on which the heart catches.

This distance of the theme gives to the style its consciousness — more of Heine than of Burns there. His world was no longer one with the things of which he wrote. He consciously chose them. Hence he is an artist. Davis and Ferguson could not have written differently than they did. Their theme was appointed by those old spinners, the Fates. This choosing and gathering of artistic moments, when he has a subject like The Lady of the Sea, is not enough. We are not satisfied. The mermaid bride of Dalachmar has too little of sea wonder and mystery. She is too modern and pathetic, too cheap. One does not meet a mermaid every day, and one does not like to be disappointed.

The other long poem, The Music Master, has the same fault, but we hardly notice it, the artistic moments are so beautiful. Witness these opening lines:

Music and Love! — If lovers hear me sing,
  I will for them essay the simple tale,
To hold some fair young listeners in a ring
  With echoes gathered from an Irish vale,
Where still, methinks, abide my golden years,
Though I not with them, — far discern'd through tears.

When evening fell upon the village-street
  And brother fields, reposing hand in hand,
Unlike where flaring cities scorn to meet
  The kiss of dusk that quiets all the land,
'Twas pleasant laziness to loiter by
Houses and cottages, a friendly spy,

And hear the frequent fiddle that would glide
  Through jovial mazes of a jig or reel,
Or sink from sob to sob with plaintive slide,
  Or mount the steps of swift exulting zeal;
For our old village was with music fill'd
Like any grove where thrushes wont to build.

Wistfulness and regret ever dominant in this poem throughout! The personal nature of this sadness again divides him from Davis and Ferguson. They were essentially national writers. Davis, looking into the future, saw Ireland free and prospering. Ferguson saw her in the past before the curse had yet fallen. For her were their hopes and memories and regrets. They ever celebrated the national life. No matter what they described you were made to feel its relation to that life. Allingham, though always Irish, is no way national. This widely effects his work. Like Lever and Lover he does not take the people quite seriously. Not so many miles from Ballyshannon — visible therefrom on clear days, I imagine — is the Mountain Nephin, where the blind Lynott warmed his vengeance for years. Ferguson chose that Lynott out, and wrote his Vengeance of the Welshmen of Tirawley. Allingham noted down for us the sound of a clarionet through the ruddy shutter of a forge, the fishers drawing in their net with a silver wave of salmon, a bugle in a solitary valley — isolated artistic moments.

Besides this need of central seriousness, the narrative poems are hardly one in matter and form. They are more versified stories than poems. You feel the matter might have been

told differently, that matter and form have
not grown up together. They have been
chosen, you imagine, each for itself. Indeed it
seems to me there is only one narrative poem
in this book that has, as wholly as the lyrics
have, this unity of matter and form, namely,
the Abbot of Inisfalen. Here everything,
metre and words alike, carries the same
meaning, alike breathes of the days when
to every eye the blue of heaven seemed the
floor whereon the angel walked, and spirits
seemed to come and go in shapes of bird
and beast. There is no more beautiful legend
anywhere than the monkish, many-countried
tale, whereof Mr. Allingham gives the Irish
version, the Killarney version, for Mr. Allingham has strayed far from his Ballyshannon
this time. Far south even of bluest Nephin
— blue as a wave of the sea sucked up by
some air-wandering Jotun—away into Kerry.

The Abbott of Inisfalen prayed at early
dawn under the leaves. All around, the island
was still. He prayed for his sins forgiveness.
He prayed for his convent brothers. He
prayed for Ireland. He prayed for all mankind:

The Abbot of Inisfalen arose upon his feet;
He heard a small bird singing, and O but it sung sweet!
It sung upon a holly-bush, this little snow-white bird;

A song so full of gladness he never before had heard.
It sung upon a hazel, it sung upon a thorn;
He had never heard such music since the hour that he
    was born.

It sung upon a sycamore, it sung upon a briar;
To follow the song and hearken this Abbot could never
    tire.
Till at last he well bethought him; he might no longer
    stay,
So he bless'd the little white singing-bird, and gladly
    went his way.

But when the Abbot came again to his Abbey everything was changed. On every side strange faces and the strange tongue of the Sassenach:

Then the oldest monk came forward, in Irish tongue
    spake he:
'Thou wearest the holy Augustine's dress, and who hath
    given it to thee?'
'I wear the holy Augustine's dress, and Cormac is my
    name,
The Abbot of this good Abbey by grace of God I am.
I went forth to pray, at the dawn of day; and when my
    prayers were said,
I hearken'd awhile to a little bird, that sung above my
    head.'
The monks to him made answer, 'Two hundred years
    have gone o'er,
Since our Abbot Cormac went through the gate, and
    never was heard of more.
Matthias now is our Abbot, and twenty have pass'd
    away.
The stranger is lord of Ireland; we live in an evil day.'

'Days will come and go,' he said, 'and the world will
    pass away,
In Heaven a day is a thousand years, a thousand years
    are a day.'

'Now give me absolution; for my time is come,' said he.
And they gave him absolution, as speedily as might be.
Then, close outside the window, the sweetest song they
    heard
That ever yet since the world began was utter'd by any
    bird.
The monks look'd out and saw the bird, its feathers all
    white and clean;
And there in a moment, beside it, another white bird
    was seen.
Those two they sang together, waved their white wings,
    and fled.

Then they buried his body at the edge of the
island at the meeting of the grass and the
water, "a carven cross at his head and a holly
bush at his feet."

Wonderful legend, breathing a piety as of
old missals. Sometimes in those wooded lake
islets one comes on ancient ivy-covered monastery walls — I have one such ruin in my
mind where the ivy stems are many inches
thick — green shadows surround them and
cover them. Long blades fondle their old
stones. Century after century they are beaten
down and washed away into universal nature,
the symbols of man's age in the presence of
the immortal youth of God. This old legend

seems laden with the spirit of such a place — a legend of one standing before eternity without glory; a place where nature and God are persuasive.

There are many poems in this book beautiful as those I have quoted. Lovely Mary Donnelly (why has the astonishing change of "'tis you I love the best" into "my joy, my only best" in the first line been made?), and many another good story besides and some odd pages of old Irish mixed therewith. They are so beautiful, these poems, I have hardly the heart to go back again to their nationalism or non-nationalism; and yet I must, for it is the most central notion I have about them. Yes, they are not national. The people of Ireland seem to Mr. Allingham graceful, witty, picturesque, benevolent, everything but a people to be taken seriously. This want of sympathy with the national life and history has limited his vision, has driven away from his poetry much beauty and power — has thinned his blood. In Mr. Allingham's two-volume poem, *Laurence Bloomfield*, announced for republishing, these things are very plain. Each figure as long as he·is a background, a something to make artistic moments out of, is painted with most accurate and imaginative touch, but let him come into the foreground

and all the magic is gone. Unless he is merely
an ideal like the hero — a thing, not a nature
— he is a child to be patronized with praise
and blame. He may be playful, generous, pathetic, everything but a serious being, one ful-
filling his own purpose with himself, choosing for himself between God and the devil.
The landlord now, too! We do not believe in
him much, this ideal hero. He is moderate
not because of the clearness of his sight but
rather from the nature of his sympathies. He,
too, does not take seriously the people over
whom he rules — they are all children, the
misguided, the Celts. Yet the poem is a good
poem in its way, full likewise of much sound
knowledge of the land question. Long ago it
won the praise of Mr. Gladstone, it is said.

What a sad business this non-nationalism
has been! It gave to Lever and Lover their
shallowness, and still gives to a section of
Dublin society its cynicism. Lever and Lover
and Allingham alike, it has deprived of their
true audience. Many much less endowed
writers than they have more influence in Ireland. Political doctrine was not demanded of
them, merely nationalism. They would not
take the people seriously — these writers of
the Ascendancy — and had to go to England
for their audience. To Lever and Lover Ire-

land became merely a property shop, and to Allingham a half serious memory.

To the greater poets everything they see has its relation to the national life, and through that to the universal and divine life: nothing is an isolated artistic moment; there is a unity everywhere; everything fulfills a purpose that is not its own; the hailstone is a journeyman of God; the grass blade carries the universe upon its point. But to this universalism, this seeing of unity everywhere, you can only attain through what is near you, your nation, or, if you be no traveller, your village and the cobwebs on your walls. You can no more have the greater poetry without a nation than religion without symbols. One can only reach out to the universe with a gloved hand — that glove is one's nation, the only thing one knows even a little of.

September 2, 1888

THE CHILDREN OF LIR *

DR. TODHUNTER in his last book has made a new departure indeed. From the folk tale of Helen of Troy, transmitted to us through gen-

* The Banshee and Other Poems. By John Todhunter. London, 1888.

erations of poets, he has turned to The Children of Lir and The Sons of Turann, folk tales entirely unknown to the readers of poetry. He claims a new kind of recognition. *Helena in Troas* was essentially an art product, the appeal of a scholar to the scholarly. It was acted on a stage fitted up to reproduce exactly the stage of Greece — everything done to rouse the historic imagination. What was new and creative was the attempt to apply the old conditions to the modern stage, to redeem the drama by mingling music and poetry, to add a new convention to the stage. But the poem itself dealt always with the oldest material, with personages who have figured in a hundred poems. The mind of the theatre-goer has grown numb on the side turned to poetry, and you can only rouse it possibly by striking where many painters and poets have struck before. Certainly Helen of Troy was still a name to conjure with, and Dr. Todhunter conjured successfully. Among the many hopeful signs of a revival of higher drama his *Helena* holds an important place. We believe he intends to renew the attempt. If higher drama comes once more into existence, it will be in some such way, appealing first to the refined and cultivated and well-read, elaborating piece by piece its convention, then widening its range and gathering converts slowly among the many like a new book, not going to the public, but drawing them to itself. The modern author, if he be a man of genius, is a solitary; he does not know the everchanging public well enough to be their servant. He cannot learn their convention; they must learn his. All that is greatest in modern literature is soliloquy, or, at most, words addressed to a few friends. We must go to the stage all eagerness like a mob of eavesdroppers and to be inspired, not amused, if modern drama is to be anything else than a muddy torrent of shallow realism.

In some such mood did Goethe draw people to his Weimar stage, forbidding even applause, and great dramas were enacted there — his own, Schiller's and others' — till they were superseded one day by a performing poodle. On some such terms did Wagner find audience. The other day Renan described his ideal theatre: it should be subsidized by the State, in all matters be under the control of the greatest artists and poets and critics of the time, enact at stated intervals the greatest works of the greatest poets of all times, and announce each performance to the universe years beforehand.

I have strayed far from The Children of Lir

and The Sons of Turann. Nothing could be less like *Helena* than these Children, *Helena* essentially belonging to what is called poetical poetry, everything seen through the spectacles of books, The Children of Lir almost too simple, almost too unelaborate. One is cosmopolitan, the other ethnic, falling on the cosmopolitan ear with an outlandish ring. One is written throughout in blank verse — most artificial if most monumental of forms — the other in strangely unstudied, fluid and barbaric measures.

Dr. Todhunter no longer comes to us as an art poet: he claims recognition as one of the national writers of the Irish race; as such we will consider him. In simplicity he resembles Ferguson. By right of fire and fortitude Ferguson stands alone, a singer of heroic things unrivalled in our days, the ballad Homer. Fire and fortitude he needed, for he chose out the most epic incidents of Ireland's heroic age. Dr. Todhunter has chosen so far a different sphere. His legends belong to those mythic and haunted ages of the Tuatha De Danaan that preceded the heroic cycle, ages full of mystery, where demons and gods battle in the twilight. Between us and them Cuchulain, Conall Carnach, Conary, Ferdiad and the heroes move as before gloomy arras.

N

In those mysterious pre-human ages when life lasted for hundreds of years; when the monstrous race of the Fomorians, with one foot, and one arm in the middle of their chests, rushed in their pirate galleys century after century like clouds upon the coast; when a race of beautiful beings, whose living hair moved with their changing thoughts, paced about the land; when the huge bulk of Balor had to be raised in his chariot, and his eyelid, weighted by the lassitude of age, uplifted with hooks that he might strike dead his foe with a glance — to these ages belongs the main portion of one legend supreme in innocence and beauty and tenderness, the tale of The Children of Lir.

Only one other modern poet has told the story — Miss Tynan's beautiful poem being a lyric treatment of a single episode; that other is the Catholic poet, Aubrey de Vere. His version is very readable, but over-embroidered, and lacking entirely the flavor of the original. Dr. Todhunter has kept perfectly, on the other hand, all the old naïveté and unexpectedness.

He begins by telling how the Tuatha De Danaan had been defeated by the Milesian invaders:

Sad were the men of De-Danaan,
Sad from the sword of the Sons of Milith,
In the fight of Tailtin,
In the fight for lordship of the streams of Erin.

To the hosting of the chiefs
They drew together their war-sick banners,
And said: "Let one be Lord,
To the healing of us all."

Bov Derg, a southern chief, is chosen king; his rival, Lir of the White Field, retreats in wrath brooding upon his wrong.

But those about Bov Derg were wroth at Lir, and said:
"Give us the word, Bov Derg, and Lir shall be an heap
Of bleaching bones, cast out and suddenly forgot."

"Not so," answered Bov Derg, "leave Lir the lordship of himself, to daunt Fomorian ships." At last word came that the whole South was full of wailing. A cry had gone forth, "The wife of Lir is dead, and Lir like winter's frost that melts away in tears!" Bov Derg, that there might be peace between him and Lir, sent messengers offering one of his three daughters, Oova, Oifa, or Eva, as wife to Lir. Lir came and chose the eldest, for he would not wrong the first-born. Of this marriage were four children: at the first birth Fianoula, a daughter, Oodh, a son; at the second Fiachra and Conn, twin sons. But at the last birth Oova died. Again the wail went forth, and Bov Derg, hearing it, sent Oifa as wife to mother the babes of Oova. Lir cared only for his children.

By night he kept them near him, and oft ere dawn was grey
Hungry with love he rose, to lie down among his children.

For a year Oifa nursed bitter jealousy. At last she mounted into her chariot and came to a place of Druids, and said, "Come, kill me now this plague," but the Druids drove her away. Then she carried the children into a deep grove and drew her knife to kill them. Conn looked up wondering and said, "Mother, what means that knife?" "Wolves, wolves," she answered. The child whirled his sling and said, "Lo, we are here; no wolf shall do thee harm," and fearing to see their blood she threw the knife away. They rode on and came to Derryvarragh Lough. The afternoon was very hot, and she bid them bathe. While they were plunging about in the water she muttered, pacing a Druid's maze upon the shore, and raising her witch wand, smote the children, "and they were seen no more, but on the lake four swans beheld their plumes, amazed." Over them she sang this doom:

> The doom of the Children of Lir,
> Thus Oifa dooms them,
> Go pine in the feathers of swans
> Till the North shall wed the South.
>
> Three hundred years shall ye float
> On the stillness of Derryvarragh:
> On the tossing of Sruth-na-Moyle,
> Unsheltered, three hundred years.
>
> Three hundred years shall ye keene
> With the curlews of Erris Domnann;
> Till the bell rings in Inis Glory
> I curse you: nine hundred years!

They weep and pray her for some lightening of their doom, and she, being filled with terror of her own deed, grants, not from pity but from fear, that they shall have wonderful power of song:

> Sweet, sweet be your voices,
> Ye sorrowful Swans of Lir!
> Your song from the seas of Erin
> Shall comfort the sorrows of men.

Then Oifa drove on to the house of her father, Bov Derg. Lir passed by the lake and the swans saw him and came and told him of their doom, and, having stayed to weep with them that night, he also came to the house of Bov Derg. There he told his tale, and Bov Derg laid a spell on the tongue of Oifa that she might confess what shape she most abhorred.

> She writhed, compelled with pain,
> Crying with a ghastly shriek: "Demon of the air!"

Then he smote her with his wand, and "her blue eyes grew white as dazzling leprosy" and her form hideous and dragon-winged, and he sang over her a doom of ceaseless wandering, "an outlaw of the air."

This brings us near the end of the second canto, or, as Dr. Todhunter calls it, "second duan." The remaining duans describe the troubles of the swans. The poem to the end of the fourth tells how they live three hundred years on Derryvarragh Lough, comforting their kin with sweet song, Bov Derg and Lir living near them all the while, for those divine races lived for hundreds of years; how they left Derryvarragh when their time came, and flew to Sruth-na-Moyle; how they dwelt on a rock among the seals:

> There dwelt they, with the seals, the human-hearted seals,
> That loved the Swans, and far followed with sad soft eyes,
> Doglike, in sleek brown troops, their singing, o'er the sea;
> So for their music yearned the nations of the seals;

how they visited Manannan, the magician, on his island:

Wizard to wizard, oft, Time in his cloudy cave
He met; and he could spell some rune of things to come.
And in Fianoula's ear his mild prophetic word
Breathed shell-like thunders dim from coming tides of
    death.

The fifth duan describes how, another three
hundred years having passed, the swans flew
to Erris Domnann (an old name for a portion
of the Connaught coast); how Ævric, a bard
who had sought them all his life for love of
their song, built a hut by the sea's edge where
he lived listening to them; how at last feeling
death draw nigh he went away to sing their
songs "and keep the heart of Erin green";
how one winter night the sea was frozen round
them, and in the midst of that frozen sea they
sang a new song — a hymn to God — and
while they sang the North "budded with
phantom fire." Christianity was drawing
westward; the old gods were flying before it.
This duan brings to an end their wanderings.
They fly home to the house of Lir only to find
it desolate and weed-grown. They sing over
it a song of lamentation and fly to Inis Glory
of Brendan to await the coming of the faith.

And all the tribes of birds were gathered to them there,
And with sweet fairy singing there in the Lake of Birds
They taught the airy tribes, and comforted their woes;
Till, as the seals, they loved the singing of the Swans.
Far was their flight by day; along the wild west coast

They roamed to feed, as far as Achill, and at night
Flew back to Inis Glory; and wheresoe'er they moved
Thick waved the following wings of loving flocks of
  birds.

The two final duans describe how they
dwelt there in peace until the coming of St.
Patrick, when a priest sent of God came to
the island of Inis Glory; how for six days
worked the priest, Mochaom Og by name,
building a church with no man to help, and
very sad, for he knew not why he was sent of
God:

Marvellous was his work; for great strength in his hands
God put; and there by night, no shelter for his head,
But sheltering as he might the Church's holy things,
He laid him down to sleep, wet with the rain and the
  dew.

And like the birds he lived, no better than the birds.
Toiling, yet keeping still, matins, and nones, and primes.
Then by God's finished house he built himself a hut,
Where like the birds he lived, no better than the birds.

On the seventh day he consecrated the
bread and wine and rang his bell. The swans
heard the sound, and at first Oodh, Fiachra
and Conn were filled with fear, but Fianoula
comforted them. It was God's bell, she said,
the bell that brought them peace. They dwelt
thereafter for a time with Mochaom Og, hearing mass and keeping the canonical hours. At
last the prophecy of the North wedding the

South was fulfilled, for Lairgnen, King of Connaught, took to wife Deoch, daughter of the
King of Munster. The new Queen of Connaught pined for the singing of the swans and
sent Lairgnen to carry them off. Lairgnen
came to Inis Glory and seized them in spite of
Mochaom Og.

But lo! a wondrous thing: suddenly from the Swans
Slack fell their feathery coats, and there once more they
    stood,
Children; yet weird with age, weird with nine hundred
    years
Of woe: four wistful ghosts from childhood's daisied
    field!
Four children there they stood, naked as when in glee
They plunged into the lough. And Mochaom Og in
    haste
Clad them in spotless fair white robes of choristers.
But Lairgnen curst he loud, with Deoch, for their sin.

The four children were baptized, and, having taken the sacrament, they sang away their
souls that night.

And in one grave he laid, keeping Fianoula's word,
The four Children of Lir; and masses for their souls
He said, and wrote their names in Ogham on their
    stone;
And in the church he hung the four white shapes of
    swans.

In Gaelic-speaking days this poem was a
national epopee known from Fair Head to
Cape Clear, told in the poor man's hut and

the rich man's castle. So famous it was that down to this day an old-fashioned peasant would think it most unlucky to injure a swan. In Dr. Todhunter's version it may again grow into a national epopee. There is not a more beautiful story anywhere extant; it is like a breath of morning air.

It is strange how an inspiration seizes many people at the same time. In the present century many Irish tales have received metrical clothing, but this Children of Lir remained neglected until a few years ago, when came de Vere's embroidered song, and then in a single year Miss Tynan began a lyrical poem thereon, an Irish lady artist covered the walls of a Dublin hospital with frescos of the swan children, Dr. Todhunter wrote his epopee, and, rumor has it, the Gaelic *skolawr*, Mr. Douglas Hyde, commenced a long version.

We do not believe any version will supersede in simplicity and tenderness this present epopee. It may grow in time to be something of a household word in Ireland, to stand beside the poems of Ferguson and Davis and Mangan. Not quickly, however, will it come to its own, being too simple, too breezy and ancient, too free aired, too altogether different from the close back parlor atmosphere of nineteenth century life. Its very virtues will be in the scale opposite to its popularity. Its faults will not injure its success much with most readers. People at first will read it for the story probably, not noticing how Dr. Todhunter in his longing for simplicity in all things has sometimes lost the fullness of perfectly developed metre — the sound as of smitten bronze. His lines are a little tentative and timid like the drawing in old pictures. Ferguson in his best poems, even in his masterpiece, Conary, fell into a kindred fault. In his dislike for the self-conscious variations and over-elaboration of modern meter, he made his lines often a little monotonous.

The other long poem in the book, The Lamentation for the Three Sons of Turann, is divided like an old Irish keen into The Little Lamentations, The First Sorrow, The Second Sorrow, The Great Lamentation. It is as completely pagan as the other is Christian, being the history of an implacable vengeance. The three sons of Turann are sent by the hero, Cian, to do for him various mighty tasks about the world in penalty for having slain his father. A sort of court of the chiefs had given them into his power. In the doing of the last of these tasks they are slain as he had intended. This poem is the lamentation their father, Turann, makes for them.

The following description of the eldest carrying away the enchanted spit from the sea spirits is fine and musical. He has laid on himself a spell that he may walk through the sea:

> Days twice-seven was he treading
> The silent gloom of the deep,
> His lanterns the silver salmon
> To the sea-sunk Isle of Finchory.
>
> Soft shone the moony splendour
> Of the magic lamps of Finchory.
> There sat in their hall of crystal
> The red-haired ocean-wraiths.
>
> Twice-fifty they sat and broidered
> With pearls their sea-green mantles;
> But Brian strode to their kitchen
> And seized a spit from the rack.

Dr. Todhunter has also, he says in the preface, written a Deirdre, but did not print it with these poems as it is of more epic nature. It was a pity to keep it back. It would have been pleasant to have in one book what were called in ancient Ireland The Three Sorrows of Story-Telling.

There are some fine short poems. The best without any doubt is Aghadoe. Had it appeared in The Nation in Young Ireland times it would now be in every collection of Irish ballads:

There's a glade in Aghadoe, Aghadoe, Aghadoe,
There's a green and silent glade in Aghadoe,
Where we met, my love and I, love's fair planet in the
    sky,
O'er that sweet and silent glade in Aghadoe.

There's a glen in Aghadoe, Aghadoe, Aghadoe,
There's a deep and secret glen in Aghadoe,
Where I hid him from the eyes of the red-coats and their
    spies,
That year the trouble came to Aghadoe.

Oh! my curse on one black heart in Aghadoe, Aghadoe,
On Shaun Dhuv, my mother's son, in Aghadoe!
When your throat fries in hell's drouth, salt the flame be
    in your mouth,
For the treachery you did in Aghadoe!

For they tracked me to that glen in Aghadoe, Aghadoe,
When the price was on his head in Aghadoe,
O'er the mountain, by the wood, as I stole to him with
    food,
Where in hiding lone he lay in Aghadoe.

But they never took him living in Aghadoe, Aghadoe;
With the bullets in his heart in Aghadoe,
There he lay — the head my breast feels the warmth of,
    where 'twould rest,
Gone, to win the traitor's gold, from Aghadoe!

I walked to Mallow town from Aghadoe, Aghadoe,
Brought his head from the gaol's gate to Aghadoe,
Then I covered him with fern, and I piled on him the
    cairn,
Like an Irish king he sleeps in Aghadoe.

Oh! to creep into that cairn in Aghadoe, Aghadoe!
There to rest upon his breast in Aghadoe,
Sure your dog for you could die with no truer heart than I,
Your own love, cold on your cairn, in Aghadoe.

The name poem, too, is fine, the Banshee being taken as a type of Ireland and her sorrows, and there is a fine description of a stormy night in The Coffin Ship. On the whole, however, these shorter poems are not so good as the longer ones: they are not so rich in association and allusion.

But in all, whether epopee or ballad, is the same charm of sincerity, of Celtic sympathy. There is no trying for effect, no rhetoric, no personal ambition, no posing. Their writer never tries to compel but always to win attention. All this simplicity and directness comes from great sympathy with his own creations. They fill him with so much pity and interest — these mournful adventures — that he has not time to hang purple draperies or embroideries, or consider his own attitude to the world. In this we believe he is a Celt, or at any rate of a type more commonly found in Ireland than in England. The Saxon is not sympathetic or self-abnegating; he has conquered the world by quite different powers. He is full of self-brooding. Like his own Wordsworth, most English of poets, he finds his image in every lake and puddle. He has to burthen the skylark with his cares before he can celebrate it. He is always a lense colored by self. But these poems are altogether different with their simplicity and tenderness. They rise from the same source as the courtesy of the Irish peasant; and because there is no egotism in them there is no gloom. Their sadness is nature's, not man's — a limpid melancholy. It is the sentiment that fills morning twilight. They are Greek-like and young — as young as nature. *Helena* was as old as mankind.

Old with words and thoughts and reveries handed down for ages; complex with that ever-increasing subdivision of thought and complexity of phrase that marks an old literature. It was as old as the old man in the Irish folk-tale, who, having wandered for centuries in the form of a beautiful stag, when once the spell was broken crumbled into dust and was blown away in pieces by the wind. It belonged to old England and old age; these poems belong to Ireland and youth. As a literature ages it divides nature from man and sings each for itself. Then each passion is taken from its fellows and sung alone, and cosmopolitanism begins, for a passion has no nation. But in these poems man and nature are one, and everywhere is a wild and pungent Celtic flavor. When a literature is old it grows so indirect and complex that it is only a possession for the few: to read it well is a difficult pursuit, like playing on the fiddle; for it one needs especial training. But these poems should rouse each one so far as he is human and imaginative.

February 10, 1889

IRISH WONDERS *

MR. MCANALLY does not treat his material with sufficient respect; he is too eager to embroider everything with humor, to steep everything in a kind of stage Irish he has invented. All this is very disappointing. When will Irishmen record their legends as faithfully and seriously as Campbell did those of the Western Highlands? Mr. McAnally with his material might have made a book that students would turn to for years to come, but he has been content to blow a bubble for the circulating libraries. It is a good bubble, as bubbles go. There is not a dull chapter in the book. But no Irish peasant ever pronounced English as Mr. McAnally makes him. The very same dialect is put into the mouths of peasants from most different counties. Why, the children of one county laugh at the pronunciation of another! It is a foreigner's idea

* Irish Wonders, by D. R. McAnally, Jr., Boston, 1888.

of Ireland. Neither does folk-lore like the following seem to ring true:

Near Colooney, in Sligo [says Mr. McAnally], there is a "knowlageable woman," whose grandmother's aunt once witnessed a fairy ball, the music for which was furnished by an orchestra which the management had no doubt been at great pains and expense to secure and instruct.

It was the cutest sight alive. There was a place for thim to shtand on, an' a wondherful big fiddle av the size ye cud slape in it, that was played be a monsthrous frog, an' two little fiddles, that two kittens fiddled on, an' two big drums, baten be cats, an' two trumpets, played be fat pigs. All round the fairies were dancin' like angels, the fireflies givin' thim light to see by, an' the moonbames shinin' on the lake, for it was be the shore it was, an' if ye don't belave it, the glen's still there, that they call the fairy glen to this blessed day.

When were fireflies imported into Ireland, where even glowworms are scarce? When a writer is certainly inaccurate in his dialect, and makes old women see fireflies in Ireland, one is inclined to doubt everything, and certainly to doubt this piece of folk-lore. It is far too ingenious, and sounds like a modern nursery tale from German sources. Fairies are described by the peasantry as much like mortals: sometimes a man will meet them and dance with them before he knows who they

o

are. They are only occasionally small, and even then are much like small mortals. But this cat and fiddle business seems to belong to a quite different person — the fairy of literature. I have collected fairy tales, if not at Coolooney itself, within a mile of it, and have lately given some months to reading all written Irish folk-lore, so far as I could find it, whether in books or old newspapers and magazines, but have never found anything like these fiddle-playing animals. Even so I would not doubt but for that firefly. Mr. McAnally has not the convincing art.

However, some of the chapters are of much interest, sometimes throwing quite a new light on some old belief. It is very pleasant to hear that the Donegal fairies conduct the souls of the dead as far as the gates of heaven and then return disconsolate like the poor earth-bound creatures they are. In some other counties, they have rather a different belief about fairies and the newly dead. One old man in County Sligo told me a story of a man who saw all who had died out of his village for years, sitting in a fairy rath one night. The gentry, as he called the fairies, had enticed them away into the dim fairy world. There are probably many races of supernatural beings, some kindly, some unkindly, according to present belief. It must be some quite different race than those pleasant Donegal *sheeoges*, for whom the Sligo peasantry, at the death of a child, sprinkle the threshold with the blood of a young chicken that they may be drawn away from the weak soul of the child. Perhaps they are evil spirits, these soul-thieves, and not fairies at all.

Mr. McAnally has really added much to our knowledge of the leprechaun, that shoemaking fairy who has so many treasures under the ground. The chapter on the leprechaun contains indeed the most minute descriptions of that creature extant. He is the child, it appears, of a debased fairy and an evil spirit. In northern counties he wears the uniform of some British infantry regiment, a red coat and white breeches, and a broadbrimmed, high pointed hat. Sometimes, when he has played off some more than usually successful piece of mischief, he mounts onto a house or wall and spins round on the point of his hat with his heels in the air. In Kerry he is very fat, and wears a red cutaway jacket with seven rows of buttons, seven buttons in each row, and when in full dress wears a helmet much too large for him. In Monaghan he is called the cluricaune, if indeed the cluricaune is not, as Croker believed, a quite different kind of fairy, and wears a cone-shaped hat, the point of which he sometimes drives into the eye of one who offends him, though generally he but abuses him in a loud voice, the abused one seeing nothing, but hearing the voice. In Clare and Galway his favorite amusement is riding sheep and goats and dogs. If a sheep or dog looks tired in the morning, the shepherd knows that the leprechaun has been riding on some distant errand. He is always old and withered and dapper like an old beau. In one of Mr. McAnally's stories he appears as a lady-killer.

The fairies of Lough Erne once stole away a baby called Eva. She grew up amongst them and was very well treated, and was given a dance every night. At last she fell in love with an old leprechaun. The fairy queen, wishing to find her a better husband, let her walk on the shores of the lake. There she met the mortal, Darby O'Hoolighan, and loved him and married him with the queen's consent. The queen gave them riches in plenty, pigs and sheep and cattle, and told her to tell him that if ever he struck her three blows without reason she would return to the fair-ies. After they had lived happily together for seventeen years, one day when she and Darby were going to a wedding she was slow and he struck her a slap on the shoulder. She began to cry. He asked her what ailed her; she said he had struck her the first of the three blows. One day when he was teaching one of his boys to use a stick she stood behind him and got hit with the shillalagh.

That was the second blow, an' made her lose her timper, an' they had a rale quarl. So he got mad, sayin' that nayther o' thim blows ought to be counted, bein' they both come be accident. So he flung the shtick agin the wall, "Divil take' the shtick," says he, an' went out quick, an' the shtick fell back from the wall an' hit her an the head. "That's the third," says she, an' she kissed her sons an' walked out. Thin she called the cows in the field an' they left grazin' an' folly'd her; she called the oxen in the shtalls an' they quit atin' an' come out; an' she shpoke to the calf that was hangin' in the yard, that they'd killed that mornin' an' it got down an' come along. The lamb that was killed the day afore, it come; an' the pigs that were salted an' thim hangin' up to dhry, they come, all afther her in a shtring. Thin she called to her things in the house, an' the chairs walked out, an' the tables, an' the chist av drawers, an' the boxes, all o' thim put out legs like bastes an' come along, wid the pots an' pans, an' gridiron, an' buckets, an' noggins, an' kish, lavin' the house as bare as a 'victed tinant's, an' all afther her to the lake, where they wint undher an' disappared, and haven't been seen be man or mortial to this blessed day.

Wanst in a while she'd come to the aidge av the lake whin they were clost be the bank an' spake wid thim, fur aven, if she was half a fairy, she'd the mother's heart that the good God put in her bosom; an' wan time they seen her wid a little attomy av a man alang wid her, that was a Leprechawn, as they knewn be the look av him, an' that makes me belave that the rale rayzon av her lavin' her husband was to get back to the owld Leprechawn she was in love wid afore she was marr'd to Darby O'Hoolighan.

In the chapter on the Banshee the word "fearshee" is translated "man of peace." This is entirely wrong. Feeling puzzled by this translation (Campbell makes the same blunder with a kindred word in Scotch Gaelic), I wrote to an accomplished Irish scholar, who is also perhaps the best Irish folk-lorist living, and asked him about it. He answered: "There is no such person as the 'man of peace' in Irish mythology; it is only a mistranslation of 'fairy man.' 'Shee' means 'peace' as well as 'fairy,' but this is accidental, and the words have no connection, I am certain. 'Sidh' (shee), 'a fairy,' is, I believe, nearly the same word as the Sanskrit."

Mr. McAnally gives a notation of the Banshee's cry somewhat different from that given by Mr. and Mrs. S. C. Hall in their *Ireland*. He is wrong in saying that the Banshee never follows Irish families abroad. There are several recorded stories of its doing so, one, for instance, I forget where, of an Irish family settled in Canada who are still followed by their Banshee. And one of the most distinguished of British anthropologists told me that he has not only heard but seen it in a Central American forest. It came to announce the death of his father, who had just died in England. It was dressed in pale yellow and had grey hair and seemed very old. It vanished as he rode towards it. He had since then twice seen and heard it in London.

Mr. McAnally is wrong in saying that the Banshee is invariably a ghost. Cleena of Ton Cleena, queen of the monster fairies, is the Banshee of the O'Donovan family. The great antiquarian, father of O'Donovan of Merv, claimed her for his family in a since-published letter. But Mr. McAnally's mistake is fortunate, as it led to the following most interesting passage:

The spirits of the good wander with the living as guardian angels, but the spirits of the bad are restrained in their action, and compelled to do penance at or near the places where their crimes were committed. Some are chained at the bottoms of the lakes, others buried under ground, others confined in mountain gorges; some hang on the sides

of precipices, others are transfixed on the tree-
tops, while others haunt the homes of their an-
cestors, all waiting till the penance has been en-
dured and the hour of release arrives.

I wish the name of the part of Ireland, of
the very village, where Mr. McAnally was
told that the spirits of the lost were hung on
the sides of precipices and transfixed on the
points of trees had been given. For it is a new
and very strange piece of folk-lore. It should
have been recorded with a reverent exactness
as to place and time. It is strange enough for
the Mahabharata or the *Inferno* of Dante.

The belief that the less holy dead are compelled to haunt the scenes of their transgres-
sions is universal. The good also, Mr. McAnally might have added, may be earth-bound
by some care or untold secret. In all parts of
Ireland one hears stories of mothers who have
"appeared" because of their orphan children
being neglected by the husbands. One such
case occurred lately in Tyrone. The children
told the priest of their mother's coming to
them continually. He asked were they sure it
was their mother. They answered, "Would
we not know our own mammy?" At Howth
a little while ago a woman was said to have
appeared to a neighbor because her children
had been sent to the workhouse. She also

asked that three masses be said for the repose of her soul. "If my husband does not believe you, show him that," she said, touching the neighbor's arm with three fingers; the places where they touched swelled up and blackened. This seems to be a favorite way the dead have of impressing the living with their reality. In the Beresford ghost story the phantom of her lover caught the wrist of Lady Beresford and it withered. In parts of Ireland these earth-bound souls are compelled to obey the living. A man at Ballysodare, a Sligo village not far from Colo[ooney, said once to me: "The stable boy up at Mrs. G——'s there met the master going round the yards after he had been two days dead, and told him to be away with him to the lighthouse, and haunt that; and there he is far out to sea still, sir. Mrs. G—— was that mad about it she dismissed the boy."

The lighthouse is a very desolate one. The ghost must have a bad time of it on windy nights. Those who die suddenly very often are said to become haunting ghosts, or *thiv-ishes*, as they call them in Gaelic. Mr. McAn-ally tells a pathetic tale about such a one. There was a pretty girl who was drowned tragically at Cashel. She was trying to escape from her father, who was bringing her away to make her marry a rich farmer whom she did not love. When she was struggling to escape from her father's grasp, the bank of a stream gave way and they were both drowned. There was a great wake and funeral, but her own true lover, the one her father did not wish her to marry, did not go to either: he sat as in a dream. At last he went to his mother, and told her that Nora, the dead girl, had come to him and laid her hand on his brow and said, "Come to Cashel, Paddy dear, and be wid me." He went thither. On the rocks of Cashel he tended Nora's grave, and then because they were buried near her, all the graves. In the day time he used to hide and sleep, at night to walk up and down in the chapel with her spirit. He had no friends, but the people used to leave potatoes and bread where he would find them. On these he lived. He was sixty years on the rock. When there was a burying he would sometimes show himself in the daytime and say, "You have brought me another friend."

When he got owld, an' where he cud look into the other worruld, Nora came ivery night an' brought more wid her, sper'ts av kings an' bishops that rest on Cashel, an' ther's thim that's seen the owld man walkin' in Cormac's Chapel, Nora holdin' him up an' him discoorsin' wid the mighty dead. They found him wan day, cowld an' still, on Nora's grave, an' laid him be her side, God rest his sowl, an' there he slapes to-day, God be good to him.

They said he was only a poor owld innocent, but all is aqualized, an' thim that's despised some- times have betther comp'ny among the angels than that of mortials.

Mr. McAnally tells this story very well. His phrasing is usually genuinely Irish, though the pronunciations be too often, as we have said, stage Irish. "Mighty dead" is, however, surely not good Irish at all but modern poetic. It is notable that the girl was drowned. There is something mysterious about the ghosts of the drowned that I do not well know. They seem to have a more intense life in them than other ghosts, or to be under the power of the fairies, or in some other way distinguished among the commonality of ghosts. It is said to be unlucky to have much to do with the drowned. Drowned cattle are sometimes sup- posed to be carried away by the fairies.

In one way Mr. McAnally does take his legends more seriously than Croker and his school did: he never rationalizes; he has no theories, and why should he? The Irish peas- ant believes the whole world to be full of spirits, but then the most distinguished men have thought not otherwise. Newspapers have lately assured us that Lord Tennyson believes the soul may leave the body, for a time, and communicate with the spirits of the dead. The Irish peasant and most serene of Englishmen are at one. Tradition is always the same. The earliest poet of India and the Irish peasant in his hovel nod to each other across the ages, and are in perfect agreement. There are two boats going to sea. In which shall we sail? There is the little boat of science. Every century a new little boat of science starts and is shipwrecked; and yet again another puts forth, gaily laughing at its predecessors. Then there is the great galleon of tradition, and on board it travel the great poets and dreamers of the past. It was built long ago, nobody remembers when. From its masthead flies the motto, *semper eadem.*

July 7, 1889

A SCHOLAR POET *

IN VICTOR HUGO's *Shakespeare* occur these sentences: "'He is sober, discreet, temperate. He can be trusted.' Is this the description of a domestic? No; of a poet." In these words the greatest modern representative of that

* Wordsworth's Grave and Other Poems. By William Watson. London, 1890.

school of poets that looks upon poetry as a direct message from the Most High, and amenable to no law but its own, poured out his scorn on those critics who consider it a purely human art, a criticism of life by subtle and refined thinkers. When Ezekiel lay upon his side and ate dung in order, as Blake says, to make men believe that there is an infinite in all things, he belonged to the first school. When Matthew Arnold defined God as "a something not ourselves that makes for righteousness," he exemplified, as always in his writings, the opposite habit of mind. It is not necessary to debate the point at issue. It would take many pages. Perhaps one would not be far from some truth bearing on the matter in saying that as nature has night and day, action and repose, light and shadow, so the mind of man has two kinds of shepherds: the poets who rouse and trouble, the poets who hush and console. It is often pleasant to turn to the latter; to turn, when bewildered by the gigantic, to men who have nothing extravagant, exuberant, mystical; to turn from the inspired to the accomplished. For most men the divine fire glows in regions of unstable equilibrium. They cannot rest there.

Among the younger men who follow the Matthew Arnold tradition, there is not one who has produced more scholar-like and accomplished poetry than an almost unknown writer, William Watson. In technique it is perfect. No ill-chosen word ever jangles its serene and solemn meditation. No diffuseness dims its slow, burning fire — a fire that will not warm our hearths, but gives a thin flame, good to read by for a little, when wearied by some more potent influence.

I first heard of William Watson about five years ago. A friend, Professor Dowden, I think, lent me a little book of quatrains, *Epigrams* it was somewhat misnamed, there being nothing epigrammatic in the ordinary sense of the word about them — no vivacity, no sharpness in their deliberate art. The book, I was told, had made illustrious friends. Dante Gabriel Rossetti had praised it, and a certain famous hedonist had written a letter on scented note paper to say it was "the most perfect book that had come from any press for twenty years," or some such words. The book seemed all the more attractive, perhaps, because, praised by the many among the few, it had not made even a few friends among the many. It was a scholar's book, and would perforce remain so. To know it at all implied almost a knowledge of signs and passwords — membership of some mysterious scholars'

Brotherhood of the Rose. Before long I knew its hundred quatrains by heart, and do not find they have lost anything in five years. It still seems to me more beautiful than any other work of its author's.

At odd times these last five years William Watson's name has reached the more alert among us. At the time of General Gordon's death he contributed to The National Review a series of sonnets, written from the Conservative point of view, that were hailed by an evening Tory paper as the greatest political poetry since Milton. In slow moving, stately rhetoric they lamented the fate of Gordon and his men, telling how their dust was

> Grown
> A portion of the fiery sands abhorred;

cast elaborate invective against all whom their author believed to be the enemies of England — Russia and the like; grew wroth with cosmopolitans, proclaiming their author's pride in "Insularity," his loving care for men of whom he can say:

> Born of my mother England's mighty womb,
>   Nursed on my mother England's mighty knees,
> And lull'd as I was lull'd in glory and gloom
>   With cradle song of her protecting seas.

It was clearly scholars' politics. He would have written quite otherwise if Wordsworth and Milton had not written political sonnets before him. The thought and feeling were in no way new or personal, nor are they at any time throughout his poems.

A little later, one heard he had finished for the same review a poem on Wordsworth's grave, but kept it back for polish. Two years passed, and he was still polishing it. Last year it appeared, and has now been followed by a thin octavo, Number Three of Unwin's Cameo Series, containing a general selection of his poems, with the Wordsworth's Grave as title poem. I do not think it has been much reviewed as yet, but it is certainly finding a welcome among that small circle of people — may their shadows never grow less — who still find time to read poetry by new writers.

As one turns over the pages, and catches sight of page after page devoted to metrical criticism of Shelley and Wordsworth, and Landor and Keats, or lights on an epigram comparing Marlowe and Shakespeare, or weaving metaphors for the play of *King Lear*, one sees at once that the book has sprung from the critical rather than the creative imagination. For this writer a scholar and his scholarly feelings are the microcosm, and the books he reads make up the whole of it; and the books he reads include by no means even the entire world of letters. He is insular, as his sonnet puts it. For him Goethe's "proud, elaborate calm," as he calls it, means less than "Byron's fire," and France has little to please him with her "Hugo-flare against the night." Among modern English writers, Wordsworth is the one he loves. In his own work he is no less deliberate than the sage of Rydal: no emotion is ever extreme; no belief is held immoderately, unless it be Tory patriotism; no violent emotion ever tips the beam of his balance. I turn to the section containing twenty "epigrams," selected from his first book, and find his evident ideal in the very first:

> 'Tis human fortune's happiest height to be
>   A Spirit melodious, lucid, poised, and whole;
> Second in order of felicity
>   I hold it, to have walk'd with such a soul.

And these epigrams still remain, I believe, the most perfect and spontaneous expressions he has yet found, having less rhetoric than the sonnets, less elaboration than the title poem, less artifice than the lyrics. They certainly contain lines that should live. They are all full of style, and some of solemnity. Witness the following:

P

In mid whirl of the dance of Time ye start,
  Start at the cold touch of Eternity,
And cast your cloaks about you, and depart:
  The minstrels pause not in their minstrelsy.

Or this on Byron:

Too avid of earth's bliss, he was of those
  Whom Delight flies because they gave her chase.
Only the odour of her wild hair blows
  Back in their faces hungering for her face.

Or this on Antony at Actium:

He holds a dubious balance: — yet *that* scale,
  Whose freight the world is, surely shall prevail?
No; Cleopatra droppeth into *this*
  One counterpoising orient, sultry kiss.

Or, perhaps, finest of all, the following on the
play of *King Lear*:

Here Love the slain with Love the slayer lies;
  Deep drown'd are both in the same sunless pool.
Up from its depths that mirror thundering skies
  Bubbles the wan mirth of the mirthless Fool.

There are two poems in the section of lyrics
that perhaps go nearer than he has gone elsewhere to seeing life and nature direct, and
without the spectacles of books. The first,
on Life without Health, is weighty and im-
pressive:

Behold life builded as a goodly house
  And grown a mansion ruinous,
With winter blowing through its crumbling walls!
  The master paceth up and down his halls,

And in the empty hours
Can hear the tottering of his towers
And tremor of their bases under ground.
And off he starts and looks around
At creaking of a distant door
Or echo of his footfall on the floor,
Thinking it may be one whom he awaits
And hath for many days awaited,
Coming to lead him through the mouldering gates
Out somewhere, from his home dilapidated.

In the second, World Strangeness, one finds
an exquisite expression of a sensitive nature
and of its trouble over the riddle of things,
a nature that is refined, inquiring, subtle —
everything but believing. It is a nature ad-
mirable for most things that man has to do —
except found religions or write the greatest
kind of poetry. I quote the poem entire:

Strange the world about me lies,
    Never yet familiar grown —
Still disturbs me with surprise,
    Haunts me like a face half known.

In this house with starry dome,
    Floored with gemlike plains and seas,
Shall I never feel at home,
    Never wholly be at ease?

On from room to room I stray,
    Yet my host can ne'er espy,
And I know not to this day
    Whether guest or captive I.

> So between the starry dome
>   And the floor of plains and seas,
> I have never felt at home,
>   Never wholly been at ease.

I believe that this little book — it is not more than seventy-five thinly printed pages — is a distinct addition to contemporary literature, and that it will for years to come continue to charm and irritate alternately, but at all times interest, the few whom it was intended for. It is not promise, but complete accomplishment. There is not one ragged or slovenly line. All is perfectly scholarly, perfectly cultivated. It will interest some people because it expresses their thoughts, and some because it does not, but gives them instead a glimpse into a quiet scholar's room, where everything is well arranged, where no fierce emotion has ever come. One thinks, when reading it, of a small house full of books somewhere in a pastoral country, with ivy falling over the windows and an owl somewhere in the deep shadow under the eaves. Taking it all in all, it is, perhaps, the most polished achievement of any among the youngest generation of poets. It is all the more to be treasured, too, because there will hardly be another book of the same type written in the coming generation. The struggle of labor and capital, of mysticism and science, and many another contest now but dimly foreshadowed, will more and more absorb or deafen into silence all such cloistered lives — the products of periods of rest between two worlds, "one dead, one powerless to be born."

June 15, 1890

A POETIC DRAMA

IT IS one of the queer things about our age that with all our education and respect for literature we have no modern poetic drama. We still go to see Shakespeare, but then we have made him one of our superstitions. When any adventurous person puts verse upon the stage, the theatre-goer — if the verse be worth anything and not mere prose cut into lengths — begins to yawn and say it is all very pretty, but it is not dramatic. It is the poet's fault, he insists, that he does not like the play. He then goes on, if he be a bookish man, to explain that the Elizabethan poets were quite different and understood the stage and people like him, and that until poets of their sort take to play making once more he prefers *The Lights of London*, or *Judah*, or *The Silver King*, or *Jane*, or whatever the popular play of the time may be. Sometimes he happens to be critic for one of the morning papers, in which case he says all this at great length and with an evident sense of superiority. But after all is it mainly the fault of the poet? Did the Elizabethan poet write for the sort of stage this man admires, or understand people like him, or even use the word *dramatic* in the same sense? Read Chapman's dramas if you would know the answer. They were popular in their day, and yet there are pages on pages in them of sheer poetry, long speeches that have no dramatic justification of any kind except their beauty. The fact is the age of Elizabeth was one of the great poetic ages. Every one, from the pot boys to the noblemen, thought imagination a high and worthy thing. Thomas Dekker in one of his prose tracts describes the honor and glory it brought a man in one of the eating houses of the day to be thought a poet by his fellow diners, and gives amusing directions for getting up such a reputation with the least possible amount of talent. The knowledge and love of poetry were then a necessary part of good breeding, for commercialism and puritanism had not yet set their brand on England.

Dr. Todhunter has heroically attempted to bring back our listless and conventional pub-

lic to something of the high thinking and high
feeling of the playgoers of the time of Elizabeth. It is somewhat uphill work, naturally,
and must for some time tend to resemble, for
both author and audience, the famous adventures of Jack and Jill. He has, however, had
more than one unexpected success. Some few
people are growing tired of perpetual *Lights
of London*. I chronicled for you some time
ago the triumphant production of *A Sicilian
Idyll* at Bedford Park. For a small number of
performances — twice as many as were origi-
nally arranged for — he filled from end to end
the little club theatre. Nor did they come
with "paper," these just people who had not
bowed the knee to farce or melodrama, but
paid well for their seats and went home re-
joicing, and bade their friends go and pay
likewise. Now Dr. Todhunter has had the
Idyll acted at the Vaudeville, one of the big
Strand theatres, and preluded it for this occasion with a play of still more romantic and
passionate nature. It was a great change
from the men and women of culture who
thronged the club theatre to the Philistines —
oh, that some philanthropist would invent a
new name for "our friends the enemy" —
who dropped in out of curiosity at the Vaudeville and were good enough to sit there in the

body while their hearts were with *Jane* afar. Instead of appealing to them with a play as closely resembling what they were used to as would be compatible with its being poetry, he decided to give them something which would challenge their hostility with every line. The motive of *The Poison Flower*, as he calls the new piece, must seem to them wild, exotic and obscure. An Elizabethan would have found it all obvious enough, for his age knew all the gamut of unhappy love from the deep bass notes of realism to the highest and most intense cry of lyric passion. It knew that romantic art alone when in its wildest and most fantastic mood can give us these lyric intonations. The Londoner, on the other hand, can only open his eyes and murmur, "The man must have been mad when he wrote that." The audiences that loved Ben Jonson's Masks, Chapman's *Bussy D'Ambois* or the love scenes of *Old Fortunatus* would have wished for more numerous set passages of poetic oratory, and more audacious metaphors; the Victorian public, on the other hand, by the mouth of a morning paper accustomed to pronounce its mandates, asks for more "matter of fact" conversations. Yet Dr. Todhunter may, on the whole, congratulate himself upon having gone as near success as could be expected. In

spite of the burning July heat, a certain portion of the regular public did go to see it;
a still smaller portion did forget *Jane* and find
the shadow of old romance a fine thing; and
some papers of good standing have worked
themselves up into very fair enthusiasm. In
his *Helena in Troas*, some few years ago, Dr.
Todhunter drew the multitude in great numbers — there being three hundred pounds in
the house the first day — but then he had to
help him the most wonderful stage manager
of our time, E. W. Godwin, and the curiosity
that was roused by his exact model of a Greek
theatre, and the patronage of the Prince of
Wales, to bring in the crowd. This time he
has had nothing to rely upon but dramatic
poetry soundly acted; and he has gone near
enough to success to make it seem probable
that we shall yet have a genuine public, however small, for poetic drama, and that we may
see once more the work of poets put upon the
stage as matter of regular business, and have
plays of heroic passion and lofty diction, instead of commonplace sentiments uttered in
words which have at the very best no merit
but successful mimicry of the trivial and un-
beautiful phraseology of the streets and the
tea table. We may again—for genius can never
be exhausted — experience dramatic move-

ments mighty as the last agony of Faustus when burned was "Apollo's laurel bough," and cut "the branch that might have grown full straight," where now real fire engines driven by real firemen find worthy setting in absurd plays. When things are at their worst, philosophy, popular and otherwise, assures us they begin to mend, and realism has had rope enough to hang itself these latter years, and we have still some coils left if it wants to do it decoratively.

The Poison Flower was suggested by Hawthorne's Rappaccini's Daughter. There is the garden of flowers whose breath is poison, and the young girl who dwells among them until she, too, is poisonous as the flowers, and the old magician who has planned out the garden; but the story is worked out with much greater detail, and a number of secondary incidents are added. In the midst of the garden, for instance, is a mysterious tree, this new Eden's tree of life, in which dwells the soul of a dead mistress of the magician's, his familiar, with whom he talks and learns the wisdom of the dead people. The magician himself is more completely realized than was possible in Hawthorne's dreamy little story, and the garden is made significant with hints of allegory.

Rappaccini, we are told, has brought his

daughter up in this garden of poisons that she may grow impervious to all the poisons — the sins and diseases — of the world and drive them out as "poison drives out poison." Giovanni Guasconti, allured by the beauty of the magician's daughter, makes his way by a secret stair into the garden. He is at first almost slain by the poisonous flowers, but Beatrice, the magician's daughter, gives him an amulet that preserves him until he, too, has absorbed the nature of the flowers and grown deadly as they are. He then discovers that he has been lured into the garden to be the husband of Beatrice, and father of the new race that is to redeem the world. He is horror-stricken to find himself shut off from his fellows. A friend follows him to rescue him if possible, and gives him in the short while he dares to stay an antidote strong enough to drive out the magician's poison. He persuades Beatrice to drink it, and she dies; for her nature had become so intermixed with the poisonous life of the flowers that the antidote drove away life also. Giovanni Guasconti then drinks the poison of her breath and dies with the words,

> See, I plunge after, and will follow thee,
> Æons on Æons, till my flaming feet
> Bear me to thy pure presence.

I wonder when anything so startling as this play must seem to the Philistines was seen before on the London stage. Certainly it has given the few who care for poetry and romance more pleasure than anything for a long time. A friend who happened to come in since I began this article tells me he has seen it three times. Much of this charm is in the play itself, but some comes, undoubtedly, from the form — from the greater compression and suggestiveness that give verse its advantage over prose as a dramatic vehicle. If we had a poetic drama I should probably be more critical. I do not think, for instance, that Dr. Todhunter has a quite firm enough grasp of the significance of his allegory. He has not made me quite certain of its meaning, at any rate. He need not have suggested an allegoric significance at all; but having done so, it should have been more completely worked out. Then again, I find the conversation between the lovers in Scene Two rather circular in its motion: it does not press on to an event as dramatic dialogue should do. It is a little desultory. It contains many things that are wanted, but somehow they are not brought in with perfect success. These are, however, slight matters when weighed against the great charm of the total effect.

The acting was worthy of the play. Miss
Florence Farr, who made her first appearance
in any important part in the Amaryllis of
A Sicilian Idyll last year, and won more general recognition by her versions of *Rosmerholm*
at the Vaudeville this spring, acted with sub-
dued passion in the character of Beatrice. She
is an almost perfect poetic actress. All her
gestures are rhythmic and charming, and she
gives to every line its full volume of sound.
Her one fault is a slight tendency to underact.
She has shown by one magnificent rendering
of the incantation scene in the *Idyll* that she
has power enough for anything, but does not
seem as yet quite sure of herself. On Friday,
the last performance of the two plays, she
gave the incantation with a force that added
vehemence and beauty, whereas on Tuesday
she underacted it sadly. Bernard Gower,
who took the part of Giovanni, had all his
usual power of utterance and all the statu-
esque grace of his not unpleasantly conven-
tionalized gesture.

There is a chance of the play being put on
the stage in America. Dr. Todhunter holds,
I believe, that the American public cares more
for poetry than the English — an opinion
borne out by the success of *A Blot in the
'Scutcheon* in America after its utter failure in

England. Browning received (I do not know that this has been pointed out by his recent biographers) seventy pounds from the American performances — not a large sum, but certainly more than it brought him in this country.

July 26, 1891

THE END